Advance P

"Read this book! I thoroughly enjoyed this infusion of fresh ideas to the Lean body of knowledge. The insights generated from gathering a group of artists for a Lean immersion at Toyota provide a fresh look at Lean Thinking from a unique viewpoint. The infusion of fresh ideas to the Lean body of knowledge will bring a new perspective to your understanding of Lean and the importance of People, Respect, Spirit, and Purpose."

Michael Orzen, Creator of the Lead with Respect
& Conscious Coaching Workshop

"In this book Tom Richert uses insights from artists to teach the importance of distinguishing between Toyota's strong sense of purpose to benefit society, and the short-term profit motive that leads to a weak imitation of the Toyota Production System in the West."

Jeffrey Liker, Author of *The Toyota Way*

"Much of what we know as *Lean* has industrial engineering as its origin. Yet Lean practices with Toyota roots are *human-centered*. Nothing is more human-centered than art. Tom's investigation of artists' sensibilities and Lean is bold and surprising. It's bound to have you question what you think you know to be true about Lean. Those who bring an open mind will be rewarded."

Hal Macomber, Co-Author of
Mastering Lean Leadership, a Pocket Sensei book

"In *Lean Conversations*, Tom Richert is contributing a fresh and much-needed look at the philosophical, cultural, and even spiritual origins of Lean. The genius of this book is that Tom discovers these origins through conversations with artists who easily discuss their creativity in the Lean language of process, planning, observation and value. But for them, production is inextricable from emotion, and work is inextricable from purpose, meaning, feeling, and spirit. This dimension of Lean is rarely explored, and with this book, Tom is has deepened our understanding of the power of Lean."

Robert Lewis Bostwick, President and Director of Design,
Bostwick Design Partnership

"Tom has captured a never seen perspective on lean. This new angle of discussion will certainly open doors to a variety of fields into the lean community. Thank you for exploring a hidden niche, Tom."

Sammy Obara, CEO of Honsha.org
– an Alumni Association from Toyota

LEAN
CONVERSATIONS

LEAN

CONVERSATIONS

The Energy of the Creative Ethos
in Your Life and Work

TOM RICHERT

 LeanProject PUBLISHING

Lean Conversations: The Energy of the Creative Ethos in Your Life and Work
Published by LeanProject Publishing

ISBN: 978-0-9998783-0-9

Cover design by Joanna McGuffey

Business & Economics / Workplace Culture

QUANTITY PURCHASES: Schools, companies, professional groups, clubs, and other organizations may qualify for special terms when ordering quantities of this title. For information, email publishing@leanproject.com.

This book is printed in the United States of America.

A Note from the Author

Lean Project Consulting, Inc., and the author have made every effort to ensure that the information in this book accurately reports the discussions during and following the *Lean from an Arts Perspective* workshop in May 2017. The author and Lean Project Consulting, Inc., do not assume and hereby disclaim any liability to any party for any loss, damage, or disruption caused by errors or omissions, whether such errors or omissions result from negligence, accident, or any other cause.

CONTENTS

ACKNOWLEDGMENTS

The workshop and report would not have been possible without the support of several people. I'm especially appreciative of Joanna McGuffey whose thoughts helped develop the idea for a workshop and whose participation and leadership helped make it a successful experience. Joanna reviewed and provided extensive comments on drafts of this text, some of which I used verbatim as they best captured important ideas. A practicing artist, she also designed the book cover.

My colleagues at Lean Project Consulting were enthusiastic supporters of the workshop, and have assisted the development and publication of this report, with both feedback and encouragement—thanks to Klaus Lemke, Jason Klous, and John Draper for helping make this report possible. Dan Heinemeier at the Lean Construction Institute and John Shook at the Lean Enterprise Institute also agreed with the vision of this workshop and provided important support. Conversations with John following the workshop were additional valuable contributions.

Deborah McGee's participation contributed significantly to providing the artists' experience and understanding of Lean by sharing her knowledge from working at the Lean Enterprise Institute and a previous employer. David Verble arranged for the Toyota plant tour and made it far more impactful by facilitating group discussions before and after the tour. Karyn Ross provided several rounds of feedback on various drafts that helped clarify my thinking and helped to expand my knowledge of certain aspects of Lean history. Also, a thanks goes to her husband, Brian Hoffert. Through him I gained a better understanding of Japanese culture. A special thanks goes to the others in the Lean community who stepped forward to help by participating in the workshop—Robert Martichenko, Niklas Modig, John Shook, and Bryan Wahl.

I am also grateful to Cynthia Tsao, who formerly taught at the University of Cincinnati (UC), and introduced me to Anton Harfmann, a professor of architecture at UC. It was Anton who introduced me to Michelle Conda, who was the catalyst for organizing support for the workshop at UC. Michelle also provided feedback on the draft that was important for clarifying my understanding of the points she articulated during the workshop.

In addition to Michelle I am especially grateful to Rebecca Bromels, Steve Hegge, Jesse Lawrence, Bryan Smith, Kathleen Spada, and Matthew Thomas—the group of artists who dedicated three days in order to let the rest of us see Lean work through their eyes.

The team supporting the preparation of this book has been extremely thorough and helpful in guiding me through the book development and publication process. It includes Robin Colucci, whose extensive editing of an already heavily vetted draft improved the work significantly. Lucia Brown proofread the edited draft making more corrections than I thought possible. Polly Letofsky guided me through the publishing hurdles, which even in these times of enhanced self-publishing services is not a do-it-yourself endeavor. Andrea Costantine provided the book layout, bringing text and figures together in a pleasing manner.

Thank you to my wife Dina and daughter Chrissy for their love and understanding, and affording me the time necessary to write this report.

FOREWORD

This book is about integration. Of ideas. Of disciplines. Of our need for holistic approaches to life and work.

We have a problem of disintegration. It begins with education. The great thing about academia is that it disintegrates. Disintegration enables the deep dives, the well spring of incredible learning, of divisively siloed academic disciplines discoveries from which have been the very stuff of human progress for half a millennium. The bad thing about academia, of course, is that it disintegrates. The real world doesn't divide itself cleanly between disciplines of study, of research, of inquiry. The real worlds in which we navigate daily – at work, in our communities, at home – are messy. Lines blur, as life naturally comes at us from all direction, bursting bubbles as it forces disparate phenomenon to somehow reconcile.

With this book, Tom Richert, with his band of artists, tackles a new, tough, exciting, promising, important matter, taking us with them as they embark on a journey with an uncertain destination. This is the beginning of groundbreaking work.

Tom argues that the body of thought and practice known as "lean" is powerful but has too long mired itself myopically in the world of "science" to the exclusion of an equally, or more, important dimension of human experience: art. If lean has been stuck in science class, what would happen if it wandered across campus to the art studio?

A big question, indeed. To explore, Tom convened a curious group of practicing and teaching artists and musicians (henceforth I'll call them "the artists") to engage in a surprising experiment. What would happen if you introduced a group of uninitiated artists to the body of thinking and practice known as lean? This was the question posed by Tom several months earlier to Joanna McGuffey; the ensuring conversation led to Tom convening the artists months later in Cincinnati.

Thinkers who try have always struggled with finding words to talk about art. The whole point of visual or aural art is that you can't communicate a painting or song with prose. You need the art. The art speaks for itself. It has to. That's what it is.

But, we do use words. We want to talk about art. We want to read and write about it and so we do, making the best of the words we have at our disposal. We'd like to think science fares a little better than art in this struggle to find the right words. But does it?

What is science? According to the Oxford dictionary, science is: "The intellectual and practical activity encompassing the systematic study of the structure and behavior of the physical and natural world through observation and experiment."

And about art, Oxford teaches that it is: "The expression or application of human creative skill and imagination, typically in a visual form such as painting or sculpture, producing works to be appreciated primarily for their beauty or emotional power."

Or as Jean Cocteau famously said: "Art is science made clear." I'll confess, I don't exactly know what that means. But, clearly, it calls into question the distinction typically made between these two critical aspects of human life. If that's how words treat art and science, how about "lean"? I'll let Tom and his band of artists address that one.

Tom and the artists assign "science" to a category that many of us might think would be better considered "engineering" or "technology" or "mechanics." Certainly, the dominant 19th-20th century lens that insisted on defining the world in purely mechanical terms remains a dominant perspective that permeates work life, if not all contemporary human life. The universe as a giant clock and all that. Even when we reject that view intellectually, the mechanical zeitgeist pulls us, often unknowingly, back.

When I read Tom and the artists speak of "science" I came to think of it as "engineering" or "mechanical" more than science as I usually think of it. Science, I would suggest, is better thought of as a process of inquiry than a set of technical answers. As Yuval Harari, for one, argues in his book *Sapiens*, science isn't about knowing; it's about admitting that we don't know. Modern science was born of the belated realization that we (humans individual or collectively) don't know everything, and, from there, of the realization that a process of inquiry can unlock doors of exploration to unending new sources of knowledge.

Considered this way, the "lean as science has ignored lean as art" argument may ring slightly out of tune to some readers (mine included). Lean as I and many others conceive it is a socio-technical system, with equal parts social and technical. A portending lean system without the social side isn't lean at all. Still, it is true that the "lean as mechanics" view has certainly placed debilitating blinders on most of us practitioners most of the time.

Consider PDCA – the Plan-Do-Check-Act management cycle framework derived from Deming's lectures in post-war Japan. PDCA is usually thought of as a way of describing a simple approach to the scientific method. Tom and the artists argue that they practice more diligent PDCA than do their industry counterparts. An interesting observation indeed. One that led to one of my own takeaways from the provocations contained in the pages, which is to reconsider: "PDCA as a process of scientific and artistic creativity." Nice.

For me, the exploration that Tom invites us to join raises questions not only the meaning of lean, but the meaning and value of art and its place in modern social and work life. As Tom, in the interests of expanding his artistic side, has taken up guitar, I find myself looking for my own new outlet for artistic expression. But, if science suffers when stripped of any artistic sensibility, wouldn't the same be true for art? Does my art – unlike Tom who just started, I've been playing guitar for over half a century with embarrassing progress to show for it – need more science?

Expect few answers in these pages; ready yourself instead for a sea of questions. Tom and his artists quite literally take us with them on an expedition to explore a world that beckons further exploration for years to come. Don't expect immediate answers, but do expect this exploration to continue.

John Shook
Chairman
Lean Enterprise Institute and Lean Global Network
Cambridge, Mass

PREFACE

In the summer of 2016, influenced by the essays of Fernando Flores and work with Chauncey Bell, I began to reflect on how the language we use determines how people think and talk about Lean. The understanding of Lean is based on assessments made by individuals interpreting their observations about Lean work. As Flores points out in his "Assertions and Assessments" essay,[1] people bring to their assessments different concerns and backgrounds. When people who study Lean explain what Lean is, through books, articles, lectures, and workshops, they are making assessments grounded in their individual histories.

Up to now, conversations about Lean have originated from the perspective of the scientist. Lean has been viewed as a scientific approach to work—rational, efficient, backed by data—and this point of view has been used to validate its usefulness. The employment of Lean principles has artificially bifurcated the scientific and artistic minds while subscribing to the illusion that taking a purely scientific approach to work, and leaving art out of it, would somehow lead to greater productivity and efficiency.

But it occurred to me: what if an approach to work based exclusively on reason has serious flaws, and that a reliance solely on rational thought may be irrational? If this is correct, then limiting our understanding of Lean to reason alone is also limiting our ability to unlock the full potential for how Lean can provide a rewarding approach to work.

This concern gave rise to an important question. How would an artist interpret Lean and what subsequent assertions could be made about this way of working?

At a conference in Toronto in late 2016, I posed that question to Joanna McGuffey, who happens to be an artist as well as a business consultant. She agreed that artists do bring a different language and thought process to their work. Together we speculated that a broader spectrum of artists might well have something to contribute to a conversation about Lean. This speculation led to my desire to pursue this line of inquiry and generate a discussion of Lean from the point of view of artists. During my plane flight home from Toronto my initial outline for a workshop to investigate this idea began to take form.

This book reports the story of that workshop: its participants, their experiences, our discussions, and conclusions. The workshop was a healthy first effort at observing Lean from the perspective of the arts. Three significant observations came as a result, and I've used them to organize this report. The workshop also inspired a set of practices, found in the final chapter, to help us start the integration of an arts perspective into Lean work. Most importantly, it's given us a sense of what questions we now have to ask.

---

1. Fernando Flores, *Conversations for Action and Collected Essays: Instilling a Culture of Commitment in Working Relationships* (North Charleston: CreateSpace Independent Publishing Platform, 2012).

Chapter 1

Assessing the Lean Approach toward Navigating the World

THIS CRAZY LITTLE THING CALLED LEAN

In *Back to the Future Part III*,[1] Marty from 1985 is working on the time machine with Doc Brown from 1955. As they make repairs, Doc pulls a component from the time machine, examines it, and remarks, "No wonder this circuit failed. It says *Made in Japan*."

"What do you mean, Doc?" responds Marty, "All the best stuff is made in Japan."

"Unbelievable," exclaims Doc, aware that Marty hails from thirty years in the future, but unaware of the reputation Toyota built over that period due to its development and implementation of the Toyota Production System, informing much of what is now considered to be Lean.

The word Lean as a description of practices was first publicly used in an MIT Sloan Management Review article, "Triumph of the Lean Production System" by John Krafcik, published Fall 1988.[2] Krafcik was working with the International Motor Vehicle Program (IMVP), led by James Womack. The work of the IMVP was chronicled in a 1990 book, *The Machine That Changed the World: The Story of Lean Production*,[3] and the word "Lean" began its journey into the lexicon of managers and consultants across a range of industries. The book had a large impact on the way many people thought about, and in many cases acted within, their enterprises.

Six years later, in 1996, *Lean Thinking: Banish Waste and Create Wealth in Your Corporation* was published and advanced a set of five principles intended to explain that Lean is a way of thinking, and not simply a set of tactical responses or cost-cutting measures.[4]

While *Lean Thinking* documented examples from outside the automotive industry, for many people the focus for studying Lean was Toyota. Toyota practiced a rigor around these newly labeled Lean practices. For the early Lean practitioners at Toyota, this way of working was born of necessity while shaped by a range of influences that created a unique work culture. The work culture at Toyota enabled the company to produce cars far more efficiently than its competitors. As this efficiency gap became recognized, initially through the work of the IMVP, it spawned a miniature industry dedicated to studying and writing about how Toyota worked.

Many of these books and articles focused on promoting Lean tools without regard to how these tools might serve some broader purpose. More helpful books and articles focused on the principles behind Toyota's accomplishments stressing that principles had to be interpreted on how they best served other industries and companies. The right principles can inform the best processes leading to optimum results. It is important to understand that optimizing results, often in financial terms, has been a focus of Lean study and writing.

The five Lean principles identified in *Lean Thinking* are intended to outline a thought process with universal application to all organizations. More than sixty years before the publication of *Lean Thinking*, the Toyota Motor Corporation documented a set of five principles based on the teachings of Sakichi Toyoda, founder of Toyoda Loom Works and father of Kiichiro Toyoda, who moved the Toyoda family business enterprise into automobile manufacturing.[5]

- Be contributive to the development and welfare of the country by working together, regardless of position, in faithfully fulfilling your duties;
- Be at the vanguard of the times through endless creativity, inquisitiveness, and pursuit of improvement;
- Be practical and avoid frivolity;
- Be kind and generous, strive to create a warm, homelike atmosphere; and
- Be reverent, and show gratitude for things great and small in thought and deed.

The above principles may appear foreign to all but the most fervent students of Lean, given an impetus to frame Lean through a business lens. This is, in an important sense, fascinating, because while these principles form the core of a business culture that was the catalyst for Lean, they do not factor in our conversations about how to navigate an enterprise toward the relationships and social conditions necessary for Lean to succeed.

Rather than focus on this more universal framework of Sakichi Toyoda, many people want to understand the business case for Lean and the results it will yield. Lean promises compelling results. The Wiremold Company, in stories told in *Lean Thinking* and in Wiremold

CEO Art Byrne's 2013 book, *The Lean Turnaround*, posted these results during Byrne's ten-year tenure from 1991 to 2000.[6]

- Productivity improved 162 percent.
- Inventory turns went from three times to eighteen times.
- Earnings Before Interest, Taxes, Depreciation, and Amortization (EBITDA) margin went from 6.2 percent to 20.8 percent.
- Working capital to sales ratio decreased from 21.8 percent to 6.7 percent.

Other Lean success stories came out of companies that include New Balance, Lantech, and Buck Knives. Lean successes have been recorded in healthcare, government, education, and construction.

NOT SO FAST

With results that include dramatically improved productivity, profits, and employee engagement, one might expect that most enterprise leaders in business, non-profit organizations, and government would be quick to embrace Lean. Yet, twenty years after the publication of *Lean Thinking* and more than a decade after the publication of a host of other quality books about Lean, our understanding of Lean has not played a significant role in developing a more prosperous and healthy society.

While individual business case studies are seemingly compelling, two attitudes impede enterprises from adopting Lean. One is a position on the part of leaders that their existing leadership approach has served them well and that there is little need to change. The other is an approach to Lean that picks and chooses individual and incomplete portions of Lean to employ, often for purposes as limited, and limiting, as marketing. This lack of widespread adoption has resulted in the Lean era coinciding with an era of stagnation for the last two decades. Even where economies are growing, median incomes and standards of living are not. Adjusted for inflation median income in the United States is the same as it was twenty years ago and lower than its 1999 peak.[7] There is significant disparity in wealth accumulation, with the top 1% of the nation's wealthiest owning 40% of the wealth.[8] Some argue that there is little correlation between wealth accumulation and merit.[9] True or not, there is a perception that the working class, whether blue or white collar, is not rewarded equitably for work.

Outside of economic considerations, surveys of attitudes at work suggest that people's sense of fulfillment with work is not growing. A recent Gallup study reports that nearly two-thirds of people are un-happy at work. The report indicates that one-third of employees are engaged, 16% are disengaged, and 51% are simply not engaged. The Gallup report states that the figures indicate an "American leadership philosophy that simply doesn't work anymore."[10]

This is potentially an indictment of leadership in corporate America, as a company is only as effective as its ability to master relationships within its organization. Employees feeling unfulfilled holds a direct correlation to a loss of creativity and the ability to problem solve. Many adults do not use their creativity at work, which slides them into a daily habit of action by rote versus reflective thinking. While easy to fall into, this habit blinds us to the observations that make life rewarding—as if we were living by the ocean yet never taking the time to appreciate the beauty, power, and mystery it holds. We forget we are thoughtful creatures, and forgetting our nature becomes a drain on mental and emotional energy. Discontent harms happiness, and from a broader societal perspective, lowers productivity and prosperity.

A Lean approach to work fosters creative solutions while increasing employee job satisfaction. Jeffrey Liker and Gary Convis report an example of this dynamic in *The Toyota Way to Lean Leadership*.[11] In this example a parts stamping team worked together to experiment with improvements that led to an increase in stamping machine productivity of nearly fifty percent. The engagement of the individuals doing the work in designing the improvements and the visibility of what the team accomplished are fundamental to the Lean approach.

Armed with this data one might ask, "What business leader would not rush to banish waste and create wealth in his or her corporation?" as promised by the subtitle of *Lean Thinking*. An equally relevant question is, "If Lean is so good why isn't everyone doing it?" One answer is possibly that Lean is hard work. Lantech CEO Jim Lancaster writes about the challenges of sustaining Lean work processes in *The Work of Management*. Without daily attention to these work processes they become as "fragile as sandcastles."[12] Recognition of this challenge came early, as "fragile" was one of the terms the IMVP considered using in 1988 to describe the processes they saw when studying Toyota. The term was rejected in favor of "Lean" due to the understandable belief that the US automotive industry would reject proposals to adopt a *fragile production system*.[13]

Even so, dealing with business failures, market breakdowns, mass layoffs, and the massive social cost of poverty and discontent is hard too.

Given the necessity people will and do work hard. Something other than a fear of hard work has prevented the Lean movement from transforming society in a more substantial way. Even among those who claim to subscribe to Lean practices, the results can be less than stellar. They learn the tools, apply the methods, and still fail to realize anything close to Wiremold-scale results.

Perhaps the problem is with the Lean tools—the techniques used to help work flow more efficiently with less waste. Not that the tools are unimportant, but that these tools form the primary basis for much of the Lean vocabulary. Even the more progressive perspectives on Lean culture, under the broad umbrella of the principle of *Respect for People,* often tend to view *respect* as a path toward helping people in the enterprise better learn to apply the tools.

Companies that experience success with Lean report that it requires a transformation of the enterprise. This transformation goes much deeper than changing how things are done. It is about changing how the people in the enterprise relate to each other. Interest is growing in making changes that better develop the people working as employees in enterprises. Companies such as Spotify are investing energy in creating work cultures that engage everyone in the company in participating in shared effort and success.[14] Simultaneously, there is within companies focused on developing people beyond the capabilities to fulfill basic job duties tension created by making changes that require considerations outside of traditional return on investment considerations. Resolving that tension, perhaps even leveraging it, is what the work of a Lean transformation needs to be, and a tool-based vocabulary doesn't have the breadth necessary to convey how and why a Lean transformation must take place.

From a Lean perspective, it is not possible to move toward a future state if the vocabulary that defines it is incomplete. This vocabulary, limited by a focus on Lean tools, also explains the challenge Lean advocates have in inspiring large numbers of people to adopt a Lean philosophy.

CAN A NEW PERSPECTIVE HELP?

Thirty years is not a long time for changing what philosopher Charles Taylor terms the social imaginary.[15] Significant changes, even those that appear radical, build over a period of generations. Lean as understood today may yet expand to influence a broad cross-section of society.

One option is to wait and see, but that is not the Lean approach.

Using our current language for Lean, let's define as a target condition for our society - or at least our communities and our families - increased prosperity with healthier and more respectful relationships, with each having the opportunity to strive for their potential. This means applying Lean principles beyond individual enterprises and across every facet of society, at least at a community level.

If we follow Lean principles, this requires that we assess the current condition and reflect upon what obstacles may be preventing a wider embrace of Lean.

- Lean exists because people with good intentions interpreted sets of practices as sharing certain common characteristics and principles. Those observations, subsequent conversations, and resultant practices define Lean, which does not exist independent of the language used to define and employ it. This is important to stress, because some people behave as if Lean is an idyllic concept rather than a human invention subject to continuous improvement.

- The people who end up observing and interpreting the Lean approach tend to look with engineering and science biases. This seems reasonable given that Lean is often explained as a scientific approach to work. Lean is presented as an intellectual pursuit based in reason that, even with its creative elements, appeals to the inner scientist in many people.

Many who use Lean have never considered how their inner artist might think about Lean, or have even considered that their inner artist exists. We are taught to look at work dispassionately, with a focus on collecting and measuring quantitative information. In doing so we close the door to understanding the emotions and moods of a workplace. We are missing opportunities to learn from our inner artist, as artists largely work to understand how moods are informed by emotional responses to sensory input; and understanding moods is important to the ability to observe, learn, and act.[16]

This leads to the hypothesis sparking this workshop: if we can better understand how the artist interprets Lean principles at work, we can apply this understanding to improve how we work together and how we explain Lean to others. Lean is still in an early development phase based on a set of science-based interpretations of how an approach toward process improvement was developed during a thirty-year incubation period at Toyota. As the relevance of the Toyota *Respect for Humanity* principle became better understood by Lean researchers and practitioners, these interpretations have been refined to better understand the importance of developing the intellectual capabilities of people doing manual and customer service work, though still through the lens of a science-based perspective. My expectation was that the artist's perspective would teach us to think about Lean differently.

Charles Taylor writes about how we become ourselves through the discourse of storytelling. He states the importance of observing and crafting a story that supports deeper learning beyond anchoring ourselves to facts.[17]

From this perspective, we can imagine the following implications for our understanding of Lean.

- In a zeal for facts, absent a concern for story, we may be creating an obstacle toward the broader acceptance and employment of Lean.
- We cannot reduce work or life to a set of facts, so adding an emotive, storytelling perspective has something valuable to contribute to our ability to utilize and benefit from Lean.
- The artist has observational skills that complement those of the scientist, and by looking at Lean through both lenses; we can gain a more holistic mastery of Lean.
- Like any system, with Lean there will always be room for improvement. That Lean thinking largely rests on the singular perspective of the scientist may be an obstacle to enhancing Lean's effectiveness.

Whether or not we are aware of it, those of us working with Lean have an inner artist waiting to be unleashed. The challenge is that those of us not professionally engaged in the arts may have long ago shut down our inner artist, at least in our work lives.

In May 2017 we started an experiment immersing seven professional artists in Lean and drawing from them their perspectives on this approach to work, and we made some exciting discoveries. Based on what was learned, several colleagues and I believe the experiment is worth continuing.

Before we selected the artists, I picked a location for the workshop near Georgetown, Kentucky. We determined that any immersion into Lean should include a tour of the Toyota Motor Manufacturing Kentucky facility located there. This factory has served as a model for developing a Lean enterprise in the United States, and touring the factory would provide an opportunity to witness Lean in action.

In the search for artists working within driving distance of the Georgetown factory, I reached out to a friend and former colleague, Cynthia Tsao, who had taught at the University of Cincinnati for four years. She had maintained a friendship with Anton Harfmann, a professor of architecture at the University. Anton's interest in the workshop idea led to a conversation with Michelle Conda, who leads the Keyboard Studies division of the University's College-Conservatory of Music.

We struck a deal. Michelle would help gather artists who would come to the workshop to learn about Lean and provide their perspectives, as long as they could apply what they learned to their teaching and administrative roles at the University, and if it turned out to be valuable, to their artistic pursuits. In addition to Michelle, we recruited five artists through the University's Center for Enhancement of Teaching and Learning. A seventh artist was recruited from the greater Cincinnati area to ensure that we included a visual arts perspective.

Let's meet the artists.

THE ARTISTS

Rebecca Bromels

Prior to joining the College-Conservatory of Music, Rebecca served as director of engagement at ArtsWave, the Greater Cincinnati region's local arts agency and the nation's largest community campaign for the arts. Prior to working with ArtsWave, Rebecca worked for twelve years at Cincinnati Shakespeare Company. As managing director for eight seasons, she broadened the company's support base to provide resources for its innovative productions of Shakespeare and the classics. She has also directed plays for Cincinnati Shakespeare Company, the SERIALS project at Know Theatre of Cincinnati, New Edgecliff Theatre, and St. Croix Festival Theatre in Wisconsin. Rebecca holds a Bachelor of Fine Arts in Theatre Performance from Texas Christian University.

Michelle Conda

Michelle is an associate editor for *Clavier Companion* magazine with a specialty in the field of andragogy—adult learning. She is a founding member and on the steering committee of the National Group Piano/Piano Pedagogy Forum. National conference participations include the steering committee of the Adult Learning session of Music Teachers National Association, steering committee of the Carnegie Hall Achievement Program, and steering committee member of The National Conference on Keyboard Pedagogy. She lectures locally and nationally. Michelle's articles have appeared in *Keyboard Companion*, *Clavier Companion*, *American Music Teacher*, and *Piano Pedagogy Forum*. She is also the author of *Sensible Piano Skills for the College Age Musician*, a guide to learning piano for students studying other music performance disciplines, and *Playing Piano by Chords*, a guide to playing pop music. At UC she is head of the Keyboard Division and chair of Secondary Piano and Piano Pedagogy. Michelle is also a frequent collaborator with the Cincinnati Community Orchestra.

Steve Hegge

Prior to his current position as Grant Officer with the University of Cincinnati, a role that has him working with arts faculty to obtain grants for creative work, Steve worked as grants manager for the Cincinnati Art Museum. He has a master's degree in English from Idaho State University. Steve was born and raised in northern Kentucky, near

Cincinnati. His interests in reading and writing, as well as his concerns for literacy and passion for volunteer work influenced his career choice. His work experience includes a year teaching English at Nation University in Thailand. Steve has authored a collection of personal essays/prose poems titled *Bowling Green Dreaming*. From his perspective art is primarily a solitary pursuit, especially forms such as writing and painting. He does believe there are possibilities for collaboration in all art forms.

Jesse Lawrence

Jesse's arts background includes a double major in theatre and psychology from Drury University. He also has a sports degree, with his athletic focus being swimming. He currently works as a Project Manager and Marketing Coordinator for the University of Cincinnati Research Institute.

He came to Cincinnati to be with his boyfriend whom he cites as a major influence in his life.

He sees himself as able to integrate pursuits that may appear to be opposed to each other, as evidenced in his experience as both college athlete and theater major. The work ethic in each contrasts, with one focused on feeding the body and the other focused on feeding the mind. With swimming, the competition is the most stressful part of the season. Working in theater, preparation, rehearsal, and learning a character are the most stressful parts.

Jesse performed in a production of *The Full Monty* in 2017. He lives near Cincinnati with his boyfriend.

Bryan Smith

Bryan is responsible for developing and directing course design programming and workshops to support and promote learner-centered pedagogy university-wide, which includes engaging in faculty outreach and strategic planning to enhance the Center for the Enhancement of Teaching & Learning impact and meet university goals. He has a PhD in English and Comparative Literature and a Master's Degree in Creative Writing from the University of Florida. Bryan's work has been published in several literary publications.

Kathleen Spada

Kathleen has a graduate degree in writing studies from Northern Kentucky University, and is in the PhD program at the University of Cincinnati for composition and rhetoric studies. She is a writer and she teaches writing at the University.

Her background includes work in customer service, sales management, market research, consumer behavior, production planning, graphic design, and creative writing. She lives in northern Kentucky with her family.

Matthew Thomas

Matthew is a freelance graphic designer based in Cincinnati. He serves a diverse clientele, including Cincinnati Christian University and Aspen Roofing & Siding, LLC. Prior to starting his own business, he worked as a cover designer for Author Solutions, a Penguin Random House company. Also known as *Verbatim*, Matthew is a local hip hop artist and spoken word poet. In December of 2011, he graduated with a Bachelor of Science in Graphic Design from the Art Institute of Indianapolis.

1. *Back to the Future Part III*. Directed by Robert Zemeckis. Universal City: Amblin Entertainment, Universal Pictures, 1990.

2. John F. Krafcik, "Triumph of the Lean Production System," *MIT Sloan Management Review* 30 (Fall 1988), https://www.lean.org/downloads/MITSloan.pdf.

3. James P. Womack, Daniel T. Jones, and Daniel Roos, *The Machine That Changed the World* (New York: Scribner, 1990).

4. James P. Womack and Daniel T. Jones, *Lean Thinking: Banish Waste and Create Wealth in Your Corporation* (New York: Simon & Schuster, 1996). The five Lean principles identified in the book are 1) Specify value; 2) Identify the value stream; 3) Flow; 4) Pull; and 5) Perfection. Each principle is explained more thoroughly in the text of the introduction and book. The Lean Enterprise Institute website provides an expanded summary of the principles. 1) Specify value from the standpoint of the end customer by product family; 2) Identify all the steps in the value stream for each product family, eliminating whenever possible those steps that do not create value; 3) Make the value-creating steps occur in tight sequence so the product will flow smoothly toward the customer; 4) As flow is introduced, let customers pull value from the next upstream activity; and 5) As value is specified, value streams are identified, wasted steps are removed, and flow and pull are introduced; begin the process again and continue it until a state of perfection is reached in which perfect value is created with no waste. www.lean.org/WhatsLean/Principles.cfm.

5. There are two versions of these five tenets found on the Toyota website. The version included here is found at www.toyota-global.com/company/toyota_traditions/company/apr_2012.html identified as the *Toyoda Precepts*. A second, presumably more recent, version can be found at www.toyota-global.com/company/vision_philosophy/guiding_principles.html as the *Five Main Principles of Toyoda*. In this second version, "country" has been changed to "company" and being "reverent" changed to having "respect for spiritual matters." It is unclear if these changes are a more contemporary interpretation, as even present-day native Japanese speakers find the Japanese text found on the first website challenging to read given the use of characters mirroring Chinese words. It is important to recognize that between the time this text was written and then interpreted, Japan as a culture was embracing new ways of looking at the world, even if through Japanese eyes.

6. Art Byrne, *The Lean Turnaround* (New York: McGraw-Hill, 2013), 178.

7. U.S. Bureau of the Census, "Real Median Household Income in the United States," retrieved from Federal Reserve Bank of St. Louis; https://fred.stlouisfed.org/series/MEHOINUSA672N, July 27, 2017.

8. Christopher Ingraham, "The Richest 1 Percent Now Owns More of the Country's Wealth than at Any Time in the Past 50 Years" (The Washington Post, December 6, 2017), https://www.washingtonpost.com/news/wonk/wp/2017/12/06/the-richest-1-percent-now-owns-more-of-the-countrys-wealth-than-at-any-time-in-the-past-50-years/?utm_term=.c4f3bda1bc88.

9. Robert H. Frank, *Success and Luck* (Princeton: Princeton University Press, 2016), 62-67. Frank compares career success to a competition with a large contestant pool. With small contestant pools, such as in professional sports wherein there are a limited number of qualified competitors, hard work and talent are extremely important factors of success and luck less so. With large contestant pools, such as in a large nation's economy, there are many more competitors and luck plays a much larger role in creating success and by extension, wealth disparity between people with similar talents and work ethics.

10. Available on Gallup.com, *State of the American Workplace.* Gallup used data collected in 2015 and 2016 to develop this report.

11. Jeffrey K. Liker and Gary L. Convis, *The Toyota Way to Lean Leadership* (New York: McGraw-Hill, 2012), 130-131.

12. Jim Lancaster, with Emily Adams, *The Work of Management* (Cambridge: Lean Enterprise Institute, 2017).

13. Jim Womack, "Twenty-five Years of 'Lean'" as included in *Gemba Walks,* 2nd ed. (Cambridge: Lean Enterprise Institute, 2013).

14. Cliff Hazell from Spotify addressed this subject during an address to the 2017 Lean Coaching Summit in Austin.

15. Charles Taylor, *Modern Social Imaginaries* (Durham: Duke University Press, 2004), 23.

16. Gloria P. Flores, *Learning to Learn and the Navigation of Moods* (Lexington: Gloria P. Flores, 2016), 19-20.

17. Charles Taylor, *The Language Animal* (Cambridge: The Belknap Press of Harvard University Press, 2016), 291-298.

Chapter 2

The Experiment

HYPOTHESIS

The hypothesis for this workshop was that we would learn something new about what people call Lean thinking, Lean principles, or more simply Lean. "Something new" has been challenged by several people as an overly broad expectation, however, if we had entered the workshop with specific expectations for results, as observers we may have influenced the participants toward those results, or only observed those comments that confirmed our biases. Our intent was to conduct the workshop with minds completely open to any direction the artists took the conversation. We suspected these artists would, even with a relatively brief introduction to Lean, see something that is invisible to those of us who practice Lean as a scientific approach to work.

The experiment ran as a three-day immersion into Lean with a running discussion about Lean from an arts perspective during those three days. While three days is not much time to understand Lean in its entirety—even a lifelong journey of learning cannot suffice—we believed that having the artists spend this time in discussion with professionals who coach others in Lean practices would provide a sufficient orientation. And we hoped that in turn, this orientation would unveil aspects of Lean that a scientific and reason-based perspective cannot illuminate.

WORKSHOP AGENDA

Day 1

The first day included discussions with several Lean guides. In the morning the group met via videoconference with Robert Martichenko and Karyn Ross. This was followed by a viewing and discussion of the Lean Enterprise Institute's _Lean Transformation Framework_ video.[1] The last part of the morning the group experienced a production simulation that demonstrated the impact of Lean practices on productivity. After lunch, the artists watched a video of a TEDxUmeå presentation by Niklas Modig, _The Efficiency Paradox,_[2] and then spoke with Niklas via videoconference. Next the artists and I discussed my perspective of Lean in the project-driven world of the building industry. This was followed by a videoconference discussion with Bryan Wahl discussing his experience learning to use Lean practices as an architect over the previous fifteen months. We ended the day with another simulation; this one designed to demonstrate the impact of variation on production. [Figures 2.1, 2.2, 2.3]

Figure 2.1 – Day 1 of the Workshop

Figure 2.2

Figures 2.3

Day 2

The second day began with the artists watching another Niklas Modig presentation, *Lean on Yourself*,[3] and a Lean Enterprise Institute video describing Lean innovation in the automotive industry over the past one hundred years.[4] They then boarded a bus and headed to Georgetown where they met with David Verble, a performance improvement consultant and former human resource development manager for Toyota. David provided guidance to the artists on how to observe what was happening in the Toyota factory. This orientation was valuable in equipping the group to better appreciate the processes they witnessed. [Figure 2.4]

Figure 2.4 – David Verble leading tour discussion

The tour taken by the group was the standard tour that Toyota provides to the public. The tour lasts approximately one hour, beginning with a short video introducing the history of the facility. The main element of the tour is a ride through parts of the facility on a tram. A guide provides continuous narration describing what people are observing as the tram passes through different sections of the assembly process. While there is not an opportunity to ask questions during the

Figure 2.5 - Workshop team following the Toyota plant tour

tour, there was an effort to be thorough in integrating how Toyota's production philosophy is playing out in the work environment. [Figure 2.5]

Following the tour the group met with David again, this time to discuss their observations. It was also an opportunity for them to ask questions about how their observations fit with Toyota's philosophy and how that related to Lean. This discussion was especially valuable for the experiment as it allowed the artists to connect a description of the Lean approach to work to how it impacted people in the plant.

Day 3

Day three began with a discussion between the artists and John Shook, Executive Chairman of the Lean Enterprise Institute and a former senior manager for Toyota in Japan and the United States. Deb McGee had briefed John on the experiences of the previous two days, and he led a discussion on Lean with an in-depth awareness of the conversation we had been having with the artists since the beginning of the workshop. One of John's slides served as a catalyst for an extended conversation on the roots of Lean thinking and its subsequent diffusion in the way it has been practiced following a thirty-year incubation period at Toyota. That conversation informed the core of the observation reported in chapter 5. [Figure 2.6]

Following the discussion with John, the balance of the day was a moderated discussion designed to capture the artists' perspectives on Lean. Joanna McGuffey led the artists through this discussion using the LEGO® SERIOUS PLAY® methodology.[5] Joanna designed the series of questions posed to the artists so as to extract ideas formed from the experience of the workshop. The ideas coming from this moderated

Figure 2.6 – Conversation with John Shook

Figure 2.7 - LEGO® SERIOUS PLAY® facilitated thinking

Figure 2.8 - Joanna McGuffey leading the Day 3 discussion

Figure 2.9 - Building a shared perspective on Lean

discussion, supplemented by the earlier workshop conversations, form the basis for the observations in this book regarding the artists' perspectives on Lean. [Figures 2.7, 2.8. 2.9]

Before going to those observations it is important to meet the people who helped to immerse the artists in Lean thinking and led them in reflecting upon and voicing their perspectives.

LEAN GUIDES

Robert Martichenko

Robert's entire career has been committed to third party logistics. Beginning his journey in transportation and warehousing, Robert has spent over twenty years learning and implementing Lean and operational excellence with a focus on end-to-end supply chain management. Early in his career, Robert recognized the unmet logistics needs of Lean manufacturers. A globally recognized thought leader in Lean thinking and end-to-end supply chain management, Robert is a senior instructor for the Lean Enterprise Institute and the Georgia Tech Supply Chain & Logistics Institute. Robert has written several business books, two of which were awarded the prestigious Shingo Research Award. He recently co-authored *Discovering Hidden Profit*, detailing an operational framework that connects the four core processes of business strategy, product life-cycle management, sales and marketing, and supply-chain operations in order to maximize customer value at the lowest possible total cost.

Deborah McGee

Deb is responsible for all aspects of onsite education programs for the Lean Enterprise Institute (LEI) including speaking engagements, standard and customized training programs, and other activities to support onsite capability development. Prior to joining LEI, Deb served as a project manager for thirteen years with a Boston-based manufacturing and technology company. She brings a practical understanding of Lean thinking and application having contributed to enterprise and shop floor process improvements, product line development, and organizational growth through teamwork and complex problem solving.

Joanna McGuffey

Joanna founded Unconventional Works to help people invest deeper in their organization's mission to experience greater fulfillment out of being part of a team through deeper, more complete thinking and daily contribution. Joanna helps workplace teams increase morale and productivity. She also facilitates leadership teams to help define and empower their company culture, believing it ripples far beyond its leadership. It reaches throughout the organization to clients and beyond. Joanna is a Certified Facilitator of the LEGO® SERIOUS PLAY® methodology and provides workshops designed to fit specific challenges, including understanding the perspective artists have toward Lean thinking. She has degrees in fine arts and psychology from California State University, and her experience includes work as an art instructor across many sectors. She is the founder of an alternative art school for children in northern Virginia providing deeper learning and experience and specializing in serving children who typically do not conform to the standard classroom expectations.

Niklas Modig

Niklas is a researcher at the Center for Innovation and Operations Management at the Stockholm School of Economics and is one of the leading authorities on Lean and operational excellence. He has lived for extended periods in Japan and he reads, writes, and speaks Japanese fluently. From 2006 to 2008, Niklas was a visiting researcher at the Center of Excellence – Manufacturing Management Research Center at University of Tokyo where, together with professor Takahiro Fujimoto who is the leading Toyota researcher of all time, he was granted an unprecedented level of access and conducted an in-depth study of Toyota Motor Corporation's most high-performing service systems.

Tom Richert

Tom began his work with Lean principles in 2000. In addition to using Lean approaches on specific projects, he also helped develop and deliver a corporate-wide Lean training program for a large construction management firm. He has brought Lean into his experience as a project manager on building projects in New England and California. As a Lean coach, he has guided leadership and project teams throughout the United States to implement a Lean transformation of management and leadership practices. Tom has also worked as the lead cost estimator for a multi-billion dollar water and wastewater infrastructure development program, and presented his findings from a number of research projects on using a Lean approach in public transit to several international transportation conferences.

Karyn Ross

Karyn is a purpose-driven consultant and Lean coach, and the co-author of *The Toyota Way to Service Excellence: Lean Transformation in Service Organizations*. She has taught organizations in sectors such as financial services, HR, transportation, and retail how to combine creativity with Toyota Way principles and tools to make sure that every customer receives exactly what they want, when they want it, the first time. She is passionate about teaching teams how to use creativity to discover and deliver the solutions that satisfy customers on an ongoing basis. A practicing artist, with an MFA in Sculpture, Karyn's specialty is developing a team's creativity and critical thinking skills so that they can continuously solve problems and innovate—a powerful combination for delivering service excellence.

John Shook

John is recognized as a true sensei who enthusiastically shares his knowledge and insights within the Lean community and with those who have not yet made the leap to Lean. John learned about Lean management while working for Toyota for nearly eleven years in Japan and the United States, helping it transfer production, engineering, and management systems from Japan to New United Motor Manufacturing, Inc. (NUMMI) and subsequently to other operations around the world. While at Toyota's headquarters, he became the company's first American kacho (manager) in Japan. His last position with Toyota was as senior American manager with the Toyota Supplier Support Center in Lexington, KY, assisting North American companies implementing the Toyota Production System. As co-author of _Learning to See,_ John helped introduce the world to value-stream mapping. John also co-authored _Kaizen Express_, a bi-lingual manual of the essential concepts and tools of the Toyota Production System. In his latest book, _Managing to Learn_, he describes the A3 management process at the heart of Lean management and leadership. John is an industrial anthropologist with a bachelor's degree from the University of Tennessee, a master's degree from the University of Hawaii, and is a graduate of the Japan-America Institute of Management Science. He is the former director of the University of Michigan Japan Technological Management Program, and a faculty member of the University's Industrial and Operations Engineering department. John is a sought-after conference keynoter who has been interviewed on Lean management by National Public Radio, _Bloomberg News, The Wall Street Journal, Entrepreneur,_ and numerous trade publications.

David Verble

David has been a performance improvement consultant and leadership coach since 2000. Prior to that, he worked for Toyota in North America for fourteen years, first as an internal change agent and later as a manager of human resource development at the plant and North American levels. He has been on the workshop faculty of the Lean Enterprise Institute for eleven years and has done presentations and workshops to support a number of the LEI affiliates in the Lean Global Network. David has facilitated clients in manufacturing, healthcare, finance, and higher education in North America, Europe, Asia, and Australia. His work focuses on supporting clients in process improvement, development of Lean management systems and practices, strategic thinking and problem solving, and leadership coaching for managers and executives. David is a partner in the Lean Transformation Group and is based in Lexington, Kentucky.

Bryan Wahl

A practicing architect, Bryan enjoys putting things together, creating stories, and teaching others to reach their goals. The design process inspires him to create, going beyond the building and shaping the environment. As a good listener, he absorbs and analyzes information first and then translates it into a design. By leading conversations through which designs are conceptualized, refined, and developed, participants uncover details and gain clarity to achieve desired outcomes. Bryan has been leading the design effort on his firm's first Lean project, which is also the first Integrated Project Delivery project for the Cleveland Clinic Foundation.

1. Lean Enterprise Institute, Inc., *The Lean Transformation Framework* (2016), https://www.lean.org/WhatsLean/TransformationFramework.cfm.
2. Niklas Modig, *The Efficiency Paradox* (2016), https://www.youtube.com/watch?v=hGJpez7rvc0.
3. Niklas Modig, *'Lean' on Yourself* (2014), https://www.youtube.com/watch?v=El2e1lxlMGU.
4. Lean Enterprise Institute, Inc., *100 Years of Innovation in the Work* (2016), https://m.youtube.com/watch?v=4ZLaBl4Y0qM.
5. LEGO® SERIOUS PLAY® is a process that promotes a deep level of reflection and shared thinking that integrates individual insights and creativity. The use of LEGO® bricks in the methodology facilitates a higher quality of conversation by integrating kinesthetic thinking with auditory and visual thinking. Joanna is a Certified Facilitator of the LEGO® SERIOUS PLAY® method.

CHAPTER 3

I'VE GOT PROBLEMS,
BUT YOU'VE GOT THEM TOO

Following the workshop, through a review of my notes and a recording of a portion of the final day, three observations stood out as informing a fresh perspective on Lean. Before discussing these observations generated by the workshop, we must first acknowledge that artists have the same challenges and problems as non-artists. Whether we describe challenges using Lean terms such as *gap*, *future state*, or more generic words, all the artists easily related to the issue. They were inspired by the idea that they might borrow some practices from Lean, and it was one of the reasons they chose to participate.

We discussed the methods by which the artists addressed problems, and several responded with an approach that mirrors the Lean approach to continuous improvement—their own versions of Plan-Do-Check-Act. This should be no surprise. *Brain Rules* author John Medina explains that babies learn by active testing through observation and form a hypothesis (plan), design an experiment to test the hypothesis (do and check), and

31

draw conclusions from test results (act).[1] And like non-artists, artists experience their share of breakdowns either because a process is no longer working or because they are failing to follow it.

People immersed in the philosophy of Lean view it as having a universal application. As Orest Fiume has observed, the principles work across industries as varied as insurance, finance, retail, farming, manufacturing, construction, healthcare, and warehousing.[2]

The question we posed to artists was not "now that you have heard about Lean how would you describe your philosophy on work or life?" The purpose of this workshop was to seek a new or previously overlooked perspective on Lean. Whether problem solving is intended to develop the self, provide more value for a customer, eliminate waste, overcome a challenge, improve work process or outcomes, or realize some grand purpose; problem solving is the core exercise that makes it possible. Any problems we can address are fundamentally human problems. They are not Lean problems, artist problems, or scientist problems. And all human problems can be approached in the same way, regardless of whether we view them to be of an artistic or non-artistic nature.

Rebecca commented that some people think that art is easy and that all artists have some "magic pixie dust" that allows them to be creative, but good art requires discipline and focus. This group of artists began the workshop with an expectation that, in a similar way, to implement Lean would require discipline and focus. No one was expecting Lean to be a magic bullet, which is not always the case when Lean is presented to a new audience.

IS THIS A CULT?

"Is this a cult?" Michelle asked several times during the workshop. "When are we breaking out the Kool-Aid?" Although these comments were made in jest, they also point to the fact that in order to succeed with Lean, people need to accept at least a degree of faith that the Lean thinking approach works. The workshop participants saw this as a challenge—without being able to create a cult-like environment, how else could an enterprise achieve widespread buy-in?

While it's common to hear people describe their commitment to working by Lean principles with the "I drank the Kool-Aid" phrase, I never liked it. It's fine that to accept Lean requires an act of faith. Any belief system does, regardless of the facts rationally developed to support those beliefs. For command-and-control leadership approaches, antithetical to Lean, to be effective they too require an act of faith. My problem with the Kool-Aid reference is that people died in Jonestown. People thrive in Georgetown.

This presumption that Lean must entail a type of cult-like buy-in also results from the impression that everyone must think the same way in a Lean enterprise. This stems from the foundational need for people in Lean enterprises to be committed to the principle of collaboration to achieve common goals. Without high levels of commitment that everyone contributes to their own growth through improving their work, attempts at creating Lean cultures fail. Command-and-control environments (like cults) do not engender this level of commitment, thus they turn to coercion to achieve goals. Coercion is the opposite of a commitment to collaborate. This idea of *committed collaboration* without coercion is what separates a Lean culture from a cult.[3]

Some of the workshop participants discussed their roles as

administrators, in contrast to their work as artists. The presence of command-and-control culture in academia was apparent in their comments. One of the artists spoke about how they imposed deadlines on those they led, and how they had similar requirements imposed on them.

The discussion was similar to what happens in other command-and-control environments. People may say yes to the directives yet ignore them [see Figure 3.1] or find excuses for not delivering on them. In any system that involves several people, there will always be explanations for failures, because breakdowns are a feature of all systems. One aspect that distinguishes committed collaboration within a Lean system is that energy is devoted to observing and resolving breakdowns quickly before they escalate rather than turning a blind eye to them until forced to deal with untenable consequences.

Figure 3.1 – Directives are made for ignoring

We discussed how committed collaboration applies to the building industry. On traditionally managed projects, a construction superintendent acts as a *field general,* and attempts to direct the work by giving orders to trade foremen, who then are expected to direct their crews accordingly. Whether delivered in a collegial tone or harshly, all understand that the expectation is that the foremen will offer a reply that indicates they will follow the mandate. Often this is offered as a weak agreement, expressed by using language such as "I'll try," "I hope to," or "If I am able."

Of course, when a foreman later fails to deliver on a directive they knew in the first place was not possible, they can be assured that on a construction site there will be enough complexity to blame their failure on some other circumstance.

One of the first things we teach project teams when they start to employ Lean is that leaders ought to frame needs as requests and not orders; and that people have not only the right but more importantly the obligation to say "no" if they cannot deliver on a request. This usually invites a further conversation on what the team—not just the individual unable to fulfill the request—can do to better respond to this project need. Oftentimes the issue may be a lack of clarity as to what is actually being requested. However, in the traditional construction environment it is common for foremen to be chastised for asking for clarification.

When a deliberate process of making requests, clarifying needs, and making commitments is followed; and the project leadership is key to allowing it to work; a spirit of committed collaboration materializes. It appears that people who normally worked in their disciplines without regard for other players readily embrace collaboration when it is offered as a possibility. There is no need to persuade them in any cult-like manner. People desire relationship. It feels good to accomplish something alone, yet their satisfaction is magnified when the accomplishment is shared.

Still, the artists doubted that this could be achieved in a large organization. There may be some merit to this concern, especially given how Lean is deployed with our present vocabulary and understanding. It is one thing for a project team to coalesce around Lean principles and practices, however, the challenge appears greater as the numbers of people increase.

Despite stories about company departments that have made a so-called "Lean transformation," significant challenges arise when leaders attempt to extend the transformation throughout a large enterprise.[4] In addition, several departments and companies have seen their Lean transformation evaporate after a change in leadership.

This shift from command-and-control management to a collaborative management approach appealed to Michelle. She discussed the challenge of managing seven faculty members charged with grading doctoral exams. Despite stipulating clear deadlines, the grading is always completed late. She asked Niklas Modig how she could change the culture of the faculty.

Niklas felt that Michelle was highlighting a very important issue. His recommendation as a first step was to get people engaged in seeing the benefit to them of completing the task on time. Then, it is necessary to involve her team in the process of determining what changes will be made to how they work. If they can focus together on finding ways of establishing good workflow, then the benefits will be much more tangible than if a work process is imposed on them.

Niklas stated, "Leaders need to hold the focus on a goal while yielding authority to others to determine how to get there." In Michelle's grading example that might mean that she outlines a goal in terms of how the faculty needs to support doctoral students, beyond just grading their exams, and let the faculty develop how they can most responsibly provide that support.

Niklas' comments were addressing the idea of work design—the intentional process of designing the work experience. This was also brought up during the conversation with John Shook. John asserted that designing the work experience is essentially creating the culture in which people work. Such design needs to be holistic, or include fast and slow thinking simultaneously.

Bryan asked how existing enterprises could engage in this kind of work design, especially given the political environment within most organizations. It appeared to Bryan, especially given the discussion of the previous days, that strong leadership and the right organizational political environment were essential to this process.

John advised the artists to consider that it is possible to create a Lean environment within one's sphere of influence—the first step being grasping the situation and understanding what can be done.

It appeared that the artists neither accepted nor understood this proposition that Lean could be, as John described, fractal, applied at any scale within an enterprise. It may be that the Toyota factory tour provided such a compelling example of what can be accomplished when Lean is part of the initial design of a culture that anything other than a start from the ground up approach seemed insufficient.

From what I observed, it seemed that they were attempting to see how a Lean transformation might play out in their non-artistic responsibilities. Of course, three days of discussion with several knowledgeable Lean guides cannot replace the experience of experimenting with Lean ideas. These artists are not the type of people likely to join a cult.

They would need to engage in the work of observing their processes, imagining the future, and testing measures to get closer toward that future. True artists need the experience of observing and testing in a manner similar to the Lean practice of running Plan-Do-Check-Act experiments.

TENTS EVERYWHERE

In their book, *This is Lean*, Pär Åhlström and Niklas Modig use the idea that work in many organizations is like playing a game of soccer with each of the players on the field in their own tent. The players cannot see each other, their position on the field, or even the direction of the goal. All they know is that they need to kick the ball out of their tent. [Figure 3.2][5]

Figure 3.2 - Courtesy Rheologica Publishing

Similarly, Michelle reported that in the arts everyone is too specialized. In music, for example, silos have developed around musical styles. A student seeking a serious musical education will be forced to choose a specific style early on. For example, it's not possible to study classical music and jazz and be equally proficient.

John Shook told a story about Terell Stafford, the Director of Jazz Studies at Temple University. While studying classical in college, Terell had to hide the fact that he was actively playing jazz, and faced losing his classical music scholarship if discovered.

Rebecca reported that the performing arts community is inwardly focused. The interests of what she described as the broader community are not a large consideration to those in performing arts. This tendency for separating work into compartments, or silos, is not unique to the arts. It's a function of generations of specialization that appears to accelerate as the work grows more complex.[6]

Niklas described the mechanism that creates this dynamic of people acting as if they are playing soccer from within their individual tents as "islands of efficiency." This form of organization gets in the way of people working together effectively, as their focus is on a perceived need to enhance resource efficiency as opposed to enhancing the work of the whole enterprise.

The advice Niklas gave Michelle focused on getting people to see the benefit of abandoning their tents, and once they begin to grasp those benefits, helping them place attention on developing an efficient flow to the work without dictating how. It is vital to involve those doing the work in making the changes. Changes made autocratically are ineffective. Micromanaging, as Michelle admitted to doing, is not effective.

Steve agreed that a top-down management approach is problematic, yet it is as pervasive in academics as it is throughout contemporary work culture, and the perceived need to organize enterprises to conform to the top-down management approach is one force contributing to the isolation of specialists into different tents.

Another drawback to this working in tents approach is that it results in a high level of variability and unpredictability in workflow. The workshop attendees participated in the *Parade of Trades* simulation.[7]

The simulation is designed to show how varying levels of predicable performance impact how long it takes for work to flow through a series of seven stations. Players independently roll a single die to determine how many poker chips to move through their station. The play is complete when thirty-five chips move through the system. We divided into two groups. One group played with a die that had only threes and fours. The other group played with a die that had an extra two and five and no threes or fours. [Figure 3.3] Although each die has an average roll of three-and-one-half, the team rolling the die with only threes and fours usually completes the work within seventeen rounds of play.

Figure 3.3 - Not your typical dice

As a contrast a die with three sixes and three ones while also averaging three-and-one-half points per roll usually requires twenty-five rounds to complete the work. Thus, consistent performance is more efficient, even when it's consistently average.

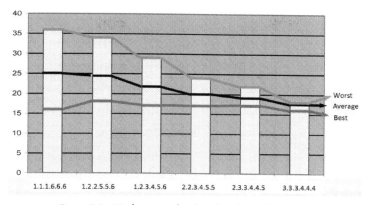

Figure 3.4 - Weeks to complete based on die configuration[8]

Michelle was able to relate the game to work in a university setting. She noted how the tenure system accentuates the dynamic of working in tents and therefore can result rolling a lot of sixes and ones when it comes to working on common goals. This is despite being in an environment Michelle described as working toward more accountability for improving education.

As Michelle explained, traditionally when some people get tenure they quit engaging in the faculty and learning communities, which causes uneven learning and often a slowdown of students being able to complete their advanced degrees. She added that as tenured people are held more accountable for their activities at the university, with expectations that they continue to grow pedagogically and professionally, less attention is placed on the needs of students.

These concerns about what amounts to an illusion of optimizing by resource rather than optimizing by flow show up in the building industry, and just about every other industry. The artists in the workshop had and continue to have experiences in teaching and administration that are in this respect not much different than the rest of the population.

BREAKDOWNS

Another important way that artists are like non-artists: they have to deal with failures—some resulting from bad work processes but most resulting from attitudes regarding work and life. While the participants entered this workshop looking for how Lean might apply to their work, people agreed with Kathleen's criticism of the idea that work is separate from the individual. "Work is people," she stated during the conversation that followed a viewing of Niklas' *'Lean' on Yourself* video the morning of workshop day two. During that same conversation Steve stated there was a need to take "a management process to your personal life." Breakdowns happen when work is not viewed in the broader context of life.

Michelle shared that mental health is a serious concern in music education. The practicing requirements mean musicians spend an unhealthy amount of time in isolation in the practice room. Deb noted that outside of the arts it is common to see people "hide" in practicing, as opposed to doing.

Matthew agreed that trying to do the work as well as possible can be a form of hiding from other people, sometimes even family.

Michelle said the term is "Practice Room Syndrome" and that excessive practice has led to serious breakdowns, including some that have led to the vandalizing of musical instruments.

Most of the other artists had similar observations and concerns. Rebecca reported that in theater there are serious problems with mental health, including drinking and destructive social behaviors.

Much of these mental health concerns stem from what Michelle termed "should be" guilt. People feel a lot of pressure that they should be among the best, if not the best, at what they do. She noted that her college will be issuing graduate level degrees to thirty keyboardists this year, and even though her college is one of a very small number of schools producing people at this high level of talent, there just isn't a market for this many people with these high level skills. This dynamic produces tremendous pressure.

Artists are not alone in feeling this pressure. Joanna said she has seen it among entrepreneurs in startup companies. They have trouble making the jump from planning the business to actually doing business, effectively locked inside the business equivalent of the practice room in an effort to shield themselves from the pressure imposed by the fear of the possibility of failure.

The participants saw this drive to continually practice as either causing or resulting in an unbalanced life, disconnecting people from becoming aware of which real options are available to them.

In Michelle's example pianists are getting the message that they must succeed as a top-level performing musician to have a worthwhile career. She wonders why musical culture doesn't make other roles (teaching, arts administration) just as important as performance. Then she and her peers could facilitate that choice easily.

Rebecca stated that if success is measured by working in the cast of a major-city production, there is an eighty-five percent failure rate in theater. This results in a constant and undue striving for recognition. At several times during the workshop she made the point that people should find working in the theater in other, smaller markets provides just as much opportunity to learn and grow, and that such growth should be the focus of an artist.

This mismatch between expectations and what is possible can sometimes be exacerbated by negative human dynamics. Matthew reported what he called a "whiplash" dynamic between students and teachers.

He has had the experience of seeing teachers set up students for failure, first encouraging their students to follow a direction from which there is little to learn, and later chastising them for working in that direction. The rapid switch of teacher as encouraging coach to scolding critic is in Matthew's experience designed to break students rather than build them up. Michelle agreed that whiplash dynamic sometimes does happen and breakdowns ensue. Office politics is not limited to the office—it's found in the classroom, rehearsal hall, and studio. The artistic life is not immune from these very human concerns.

LIFE GETS IN THE WAY

One of the challenge questions Joanna asked the group to address through their LEGO® SERIOUS PLAY® reflections on Lean thinking was "What gets in the way of your art?" It was a way for the artists to acknowledge that there are obstacles to practicing their craft, and a way of getting them to think about their creative process and how that process might relate to the ideas they learned about Lean. There was a common theme of internal and external distractions that detracted from a focus on art, and that these distractions are aspects of life.

Kathleen noted that she was always finding other things to do besides writing. She spoke about seeking balance in her life to avoid distraction. There always seem to be new ideas that disrupt her work rhythm and leave her feeling as if she is constantly spinning around.

Michelle spoke about how outside ideas can get in the way. For her it was other people's preconceived notions as to how she should spend her time, taking her away from her music. She finds that she needs to eliminate these other ideas.

Rebecca admitted that not digging into all the work that needs to be accomplished gets in her way. Sometimes it is difficult to focus on details because of her desire to keep looking at a bigger picture.

Steve spoke of his concern with just diving into writing without a plan, and said that too many ideas in his head could be a distraction.

The next challenge question asked the artists to think about what connections they could make between what they learned about Lean and their personal creative process. Many of the artists saw the application of Lean as a method to address the things that get in the way of their work.

Kathleen saw Lean as a way of empowering her work. Even when non-controllable elements enter, Lean gave her the sense that she can observe ideas from a perspective outside her own. This perspective will allow her to focus on those elements she can control.

Steve found value in the importance placed upon integrating the personal and professional selves, including the importance of making work meaningful, and stated that people need to practice that more.

Bryan saw that his craft, writing, needed to have a cause as a firm foundation. Without meaning and purpose to help define his work, he finds it difficult to represent a central concept. A Lean approach to integrating purpose throughout his work could contribute to his creative process.

Michelle saw the need to be a person who can diffuse the negative energy that can arise from interactions with colleagues. As a leader she saw how listening to colleagues is a way of nurturing team creativity. Without such leadership negative energy can not only diminish her creativity but also that of others.

The idea that people can get in the way came up several times in the discussion. Visual artists, musicians, and writers alike often work without the active involvement of other people. Matthew made the point that while he observed relationships to be an important part of the Lean approach to work, as both a graphic artist and a spoken word poet engaged in a solitary process, it is difficult in his practices to involve others in the creative process. It was as if involving other people might constrain him through expectations he does not care to address. This dynamic of people getting in the way is one I observe when coaching project teams, and one coaches working in other industries also observe.

---

1. John J. Medina, *Brain Rules* (Seattle: Pear Press, 2014), 246. John Medina describes this process of infant stage learning to demonstrate exploration as a natural act as part of his Brain Rule #12. This natural tendency—curiosity and an enthusiasm for learning and exploration —is one Medina believes will last throughout one's life so long as educational and other influences do not extinguish it.

2. Orest Fiume, "You Are Not Different: Make Universal Lean Principles Work Locally," *The Lean Post* (June 7, 2016), https://www.lean.org/LeanPost/Posting.cfm?LeanPostId=580.

3. The term *committed collaboration* may arguably be redundant as there truly is not collaboration without commitment between all the collaborators. The term is used in this part of the text because the word *collaboration* is currently used loosely and often refers to groups that are collegial yet not really collaborative.

4. Jeffrey K. Liker and Karyn Ross, *The Toyota Way to Service Excellence* (New York: McGraw-Hill Education, 2017). Chapter 6 illustrates the challenge many companies have in expanding a successful Lean transformation from a department or division companywide. Leaders outside the transformed division fail to observe correctly the people-centric work that made that transformation possible, and implement mechanistic systems mislabeled Lean.

5. Niklas Modig and Pär Åhlström, *This is Lean* (Stockholm: Rheologica Publishing, 2013), chapter 10. The authors make the additional point that the players in tents are rewarded for merely kicking the ball out of their tent and not for the team meeting overall goals.

6. Jim Womack, *Gemba Walks,* 2nd ed. (Cambridge: Lean Enterprise Institute, 2013). The essay titled "Lean Management for Healthcare" provides an example of how

silos develop within increasingly complex healthcare systems.

7. Inspired by a narrative describing a scout hike in *The Goal* written by Eliyahu M. Goldratt and Jeff Cox (Great Barrington: North River Press, 1992), Greg Howell developed the Parade of Trades game to demonstrate the impact of various degrees of variability on project completion times. A thorough review of the game can be found in a paper published as part of the 1998 International Group for Lean Construction Proceedings, Iris D. Tommelein, David Riley, and Greg A. Howell, *Parade Game: Impact of Work Flow Variability on Succeeding Trade Performance.*

8. This chart shows the distribution of possible completion times with different die number combinations based on a computer simulation. Note that the 3,3,3,4,4,4 die results in a narrow range of possible completion times and a much shorter average completion time when compared to the 1,1,1,6,6,6 die at the other extreme.

CHAPTER 4

OBSERVATION ONE –
LEAN AND THE CREATIVE ETHIC

The workshop exposed the artists to the promise of Lean as creating a way of working and living that was consistent with the artistic mindset. The artists all saw that Lean as practiced was a mindset, and they observed in Lean qualities that mirrored not merely an artistic mindset, but a creative ethic. I choose the word ethic because the participants clearly held a moral reverence for artistic work that we do not see as much with work in other spheres. Whereas a mindset, whether directed toward process or results, does not carry that same moral weight.

Despite coming from what the artists labeled the *corporate world*, many of the Lean concepts we introduced felt familiar to the group. One aspect was the focus on continually improving the process or practice. Joanna explained that for many artists the final performance or artifact is much less important than the process of arriving at the final work. The process endures while the performance or artifact is only a point in time, and when the artist observes their finished product, they recall the journey, and often the emotions embodied in that journey.

WE KNOW THIS

Karyn Ross discussed in Lean terms the process she uses with clients to make service improvements. She then explained how she uses that same process in her work as an artist. Several of the Lean practitioners introduced Plan-Do-Check-Act as a scientific approach for the creative process of taking an idea from imagination to reality. With her clients and with her art, Karyn said she is continually checking progress against a creatively imagined ideal.

Rebecca reacted stating that the process Karyn described sounded like design thinking and that this is something artists know how to do. The idea of having a systematic approach not only made sense, but also it was essential to how she and others in the room approach their work. This sentiment helped reinforce that the discussion these few days would be grounded on an approach toward doing work.

Rebecca chimed in that if *process* is what is needed in the corporate world, then artists have a key expertise that the corporate world needs. This point of connection between the artistic world and the corporate world was a theme that would run throughout the workshop, with declarations that each could learn from the other if willing. The other thing this comment did was confirm a bias the artists had that Lean is a corporate practice.

The general idea that extraordinary results come from "magic pixie dust" is not limited to the arts. In athletics there is a similar dynamic, wherein only the result is visible to people watching a competitive event and not the years of training that went into making that result possible. The same might be said of a surgeon, a finish carpenter, a baker, and similarly skilled people. Their daily work is itself a form of practicing and improving process expertise to which the artist relates.

That a Lean approach includes an awareness and focus on daily practice along with improvement of process expertise helped make it relatable to the members of the workshop.

The group reported that while they use process expertise while crafting their art, this expertise is not always applied when artists work in the non-art world. For this group their creative world—which many, including non-artists, do not define as work—followed a focused process. It was their work outside of their artistic pursuits, whether in administration, teaching, or management where they felt that processes were not in place.

This variance between how the artists approached their art and their approach to other responsibilities invites an interesting notion regarding how people distinguish between activity that is work and activity that is something other than work. Issues such as resultant monetary value, suffering and toil, degree of passion, and relative freedom regarding creativity tend to color whether we describe activity as work versus play, growth, or personal development.

Jesse discussed how artists flip between two different worlds of being an artist and being, in his case, a marketing coordinator when it comes to planning work. He said in theater everything is planned, right down to the last detail. Everything needs to follow a well-developed plan or the whole production risks falling apart. Deviations from plan need to be detected quickly and adjustments made to keep the show going. He then went on to say that in his experience, work in the business world is not planned at all. Work happens, but in an ad hoc manner.

It is interesting that Jesse and others draw a distinction between their work as artists and work they consider non-artistic. That is not so different than the way work is viewed in other disciplines. There is the work we enjoy, where we feel that we are contributing our skills the most. Then there is the work that we find we must do to support the work we enjoy, whether the work is administration, meeting participation, equipment changeovers, material ordering, or other work that seems unconnected to the value we are seeking to create.

At several points during all three days of the workshop Michelle remarked that at times "we think we are being Lean when the actions we see as Lean take away from the student experience." That comment demonstrated that she held a common misunderstanding about Lean and the messages the Lean guides were attempting to communicate. Michelle later learned that a Lean approach in the classroom means adding value to the student experience, and not necessarily moving through the process of teaching as efficiently as possible. Understanding this about the Lean approach, she stated it is important to plan teaching to address the needs of her students—effectively her customers—when she is in her teaching role.

The workshop leaders discussed a Lean approach to planning work by pulling the work from the delivery to a customer toward the beginning stage of that value stream. For readers unfamiliar with Lean concepts, pulling is a thought process that plans and coordinates work according to the timing of needs and requests from customers, as opposed to coordinating work based on the timing of available resources, thus "pushing" work toward completion to be stored until needed by customers. This was not a new concept for the artists. Michelle discussed how in preparation for a concert event she routinely starts with an understanding of the finished product she'll need to prepare for the concert and then works backwards to determine when she must complete each task leading up to it. That was in contrast to how she planned her administrative work, based on when time was available.

As another example that a Lean type of rigor is present in artistic work, Rebecca reported that continuous improvement is integral to preparing for a performance, and improvements will continue to happen throughout the performance itself. And similar to Michelle and Jesse's experiences, she noted that this same rigor is not applied in administrative work.

Rebecca, Jesse, and Michelle, and to a certain degree also Matthew, expressed a sense that this rigor is necessary to support work that is important, is highly visible, and creates an experience of value to the artist. Work that participants deemed less important did not, in their view, require rigor, as it seems disconnected to the important artistic work and had not appeared to require the creative ethic—at least before this workshop.

By the end of the workshop, participants held a greater awareness that they could apply the creative ethic to all work. This is an important point. There are qualities and instincts inherent in the artistic process that had been conditioned out of them when in roles outside the arts. This artificial membrane between science and art or industrious work and art that has been constructed during the last several centuries has handicapped both the scientist and the artist. It also handicaps our shared understanding of value, which will be discussed in the next chapter.

FLOW, NO FLOW

The Toyota plant tour provided an example of Lean working across a large group of people working in multiple departments. The workshop artists accepted the assertion that people committed to Lean behaviors staffed the plant. They also understood that the plant was initially staffed with these Lean principles in mind, and that people were selected based on how well they fit into a culture that was intentionally designed.

Bryan stated that when Lean is working, work feels like ballet. He saw the work in the factory as carefully orchestrated, running smoothly as a dance between workers and machines. The tour included numerous indications of problems on the assembly line, with assemblers pulling the famous Andon cord[1] and team leaders rushing to assist. Even with these obvious problems and because of the way they were dealt with swiftly, the artists had a sense of flow as car assemblies proceeded through the factory. They had become familiar with the concepts of flow and flow efficiency the day before, both through a discussion with Niklas Modig and participation in a multi-stage airplane production simulation.[2] Several of them equated this to flow in dance and in music and stated that artists know how to create flow, and that if the corporate world was really interested in knowing how to create flow they could learn something from artists.

This recurring theme, vividly modeled by Rebecca [Figure 4.1], that there is this wall between the corporate world and the artistic world the two sides are unable to breach, despite obvious benefits to

Figure 4.1 The wall between the corporate and artistic worlds

working together, is fascinating from a couple of perspectives.

First, despite there being no assertion by any of the Lean guides participating in the workshop that Lean thinking functions exclusively in the corporate world, the assumption that Lean is a corporate thing persisted. Second, we as a society have created a construct that places corporate work and artistic work at poles.

Following the workshop Joanna had some thoughts on this issue. The educational system has focused on teaching students how to find the right answer, know the correct facts, and to shade the correct ovals neatly with number two pencils. She has observed that even when creativity is nominally encouraged, the student is instructed in the proper paint-by-number steps toward what ends up being pseudo-creativity. The teaching focuses more on the product than the process of learning. The years of indoctrination by the system, teaching children *what* to think but not *how* to think, serves to create a mindset that looks for the one true path toward advancement. That path might be knowing the correct answers, attending the best schools, joining the right clubs, publishing the requisite number of papers, or some other form of paying dues. From a young age, children are taught this mindset of embracing obedience to a path, not a purpose, or risk being branded an outcast. Kathleen alluded to something similar during the workshop when she stated, "You're taking a risk when you think differently."

The artists expressed on several occasions what they saw as a major challenge to Lean—that its adoption would not be attainable in a significant part of society. The Georgetown Toyota plant was designed to be Lean from the beginning. To successfully integrate Lean within existing enterprises all staff would need to commit to Lean practices, and without such full-on commitment, the workshop participants could not see how Lean could be sustained in a workplace.

If in a Lean environment work flows like a ballet, how many people can or are even willing to dance? Especially if there is a perceived disconnect between the Lean message and Lean in practice. Bryan most directly voiced that there is a tension between the way Lean thinking is expressed and how Lean thinking appears to be practiced, stating this sentiment several times the last two days of the workshop.

Michelle and Kathleen also pointed out what they saw as inconsistencies. One such perceived inconsistency came out early in the workshop when Robert Martichenko provided an example of how the Lean practice of visual management allowed seasonal workers in a large retail distribution center to effectively perform their jobs despite not knowing the English language.

The artists questioned how the temporary employment of a large workforce for about twelve percent of the year supported the Lean principle of *Respect for People*. They voiced this concern after the discussion with Robert had concluded. In a follow up conversation, Robert reported that many retailers do up to seventy percent of their annual sales in the six weeks leading up to Christmas. As in industries such as agriculture and tourism, variability of demand throughout the year makes it impractical to meet seasonal peaks with a stable workforce, or sustain peak season employment throughout the year.

While the artists appreciated the practical realities of this retailer and other enterprises with seasonal demand variability, they still perceived a gap between this practical reality and what they perceived to be a Lean ideal.

There were other instances where the artists perceived inconsistencies between the Lean principle *of Respect for Peo*ple and practical examples of how companies operate using Lean. Specifically noted was a Steve Jobs' quote that John Shook used to illustrate a point about innovation.[3] While John's intention was to put forth the idea of embracing mistakes as part of the innovation process, the artists criticized using Jobs' words to describe an idea related to Lean. They cited reported poor working conditions in factories that make Apple product components, as well as Jobs' personal conduct, as reasons for this reaction.

We had a conversation regarding the distinction in Lean between ideal conditions and current conditions, including admissions by the people of Toyota that they do not live up to the ideals they promote. Jeffrey Liker tells a story in *The Toyota Way to Service Excellence* of meeting Eiji Toyoda who told Jeffrey that Toyota had a long way to go to meet the ideals described in Liker's first book, *The Toyota Way*.[4]

I also recounted for the workshop statements made at a recent conference by former Toyota employees that while the people at Toyota work very hard to live the Toyota Way, they have challenges, and that the work is far from perfect.

Asked about the Toyota safety recall issues of the last decade, we explained how Toyota had held a goal to grow into the largest car company in the world, which would be the likely result if the company achieved its Global Vision 2010 target of fifteen percent market share. In an interview with Akio Toyoda, Jeffrey Liker reported that Toyoda said some within Toyota mistook this market share target as the goal itself, rather than Toyoda's intention that hitting the sales target would be mere evidence that the company was achieving its goal of being the most respected automaker in the world.[5]

This shift of focus to sales and profit by some had been a mistake. All at the workshop agreed that the two different purposes, best versus biggest, would result in different behaviors, including the rapid expansion of a workforce uninitiated in the norms practiced at Toyota.

I also recounted my personal story of poor treatment by the Toyota customer call center when calling to discuss unacceptable problems with two 2005 Toyota vehicles.[6]

These candid stories about Toyota appeared to engender a better understanding of Lean as an ideal and enabled participants to see that while enterprises and individuals may strive for an ideal, even the most earnest efforts will fail. The stories helped the participants see that Toyota and other Lean enterprises are in a continuous process of creation and not final artifacts of virtue—the virtue is in the striving.

FOCUS ON THE INDIVIDUAL

The artists in the workshop were impressed with the degree to which Lean principles place importance on the individual. Some had a prior impression,[7] shared by many in business who think they are practicing Lean, that Lean was about making work more efficient so that people can be eliminated. When they learned that the proper application of Lean is to view productivity gains as a path toward growth this helped the artists appreciate a positive aspect of the philosophy.

They admired the intention behind the *Respect for People* principle. We revealed that the principle was not about being "nice," but rather being willing to communicate to others their own responsibility to grow and develop in their job each day through improving their work in some way. In some contexts this could be considered overly demanding; however, the link between personal growth and job improvement is clear.

We did not discuss the role observation plays in the *Respect for People* principle, which was a missed opportunity. Artists rely on their own observation skills to start and improve upon their work. They proactively participate in improving upon their work. Participants appreciated that a corporate enterprise would demand employees creatively participate in their work, rather than take on a drone-like mindset. This creative participation requires observational skills similar to that of an artist.

The *Respect for People* principle may not have seemed overly demanding to the workshop attendees because they saw it at work during the Georgetown Toyota factory tour. This came out in several comments following the tour. People were busy but not stressed. Matthew commented after the tour that Lean seemed to be about a way of living and thinking that causes us to value morality and relationships. He was surprised to observe that the factory employees appeared to genuinely like their work, and he was impressed that the work required them to hold an awareness of being in the present, a quality he stated is important to people, and yet usually neglected. Kathleen commented that the factory appeared to value the idea of shaping a culture, and not so much on the commonly discussed Lean focus on efficiency and reducing waste.

The Toyota plant has a healthy amount of automation incorporated into the manufacturing operations. In some sections the assemblers work in tandem with tools and machines. In others automated machines work alone. To take the tour visitors ride in a small tram seating up to sixteen visitors. A guide narrates the tour as a driver follows a specific route. In this manner, a group of visitors is exposed to a large portion of the factory in less than an hour, including the sections with many workers and the sections that were totally automated. Kathleen declared that she felt the most comfortable in sections where people worked. Being in the areas utilized only by machines made her feel tense.

The artists were also impressed that the company encouraged socialization by coordinating work so that during a shift everyone took their mid-day meal break at the same time in one of the factory's several cafeterias. Even the work breakout areas, such as standing meeting rooms, appeared to be designed to foster personal interactions. The workers they observed demonstrated a sense of friendliness and mutual respect. The artists were surprised that a factory could provide a social environment, and saw these measures as another example of Toyota fostering a respect for people as individuals.

The artists believed that the Georgetown factory exemplified Lean practices because Toyota came in with a well-established culture and had indoctrinated workers into its culture from the beginning of their tenure. The artists doubted whether creating this kind of culture would be possible in an existing enterprise and guessed that unless everyone in an organization bought into the Lean philosophy, it could not succeed.

The artists could cite the discussion with Karyn Ross the day before, during which she stressed the importance of permitting *all* individuals in an enterprise to be able to use their creativity. Karyn commented that Lean is about creating a culture of excellence, and that this culture of excellence allows people to do things that make a better world. While struggling with the idea that everyone in an enterprise needs to be committed to Lean practices, they agreed that the focus on individual creativity was important.

Another example of how Lean addressed the needs of individuals was present in Niklas Modig's TEDxUmeå *The Efficiency Paradox* video the artists viewed during the first day. The example given in the talk was the improvement of a medical assessment and treatment program for children. The improvement of this program, treating patients faster and more effectively, achieved far more than economic returns. It achieved a higher quality of life for families at a point when they were facing health and emotional challenges.

The potential for the Lean approach to create a very desirable human system of work appealed to the members of the workshop because there was a focus on helping the individual use work to develop and grow. In this sense, Lean mirrors the creative ethic they rely upon in their artistic work.

---

1. Andon is a Japanese word translated as meaning to notify others of a problem. The Andon cord was developed in Toyota factories and copied by other manufacturers. Some reports give credit to W. Edwards Deming for the idea of having a mechanism for workers to halt production when they find a quality or process problem. More likely the idea is a continuation of the principle Sakichi Toyoda employed in his automated loom; halting operation when a thread broke. In the Georgetown factory, one pull of the cord indicated that a team leader was needed to address a problem within a local production cell. If the problem could not be addressed quickly, a second pull of the cord stopped the entire assembly line. While Toyota began replacing the cords with easier to reach wireless buttons in some factories, the Andon cord was still in place, and in use, when the artists toured the Georgetown factory.

2. We used a simulation created by Visionary Products, Inc. that demonstrates several Lean concepts through a multi-stage assembly of toy bricks into model airplanes.

3. The Steve Jobs' quote John was citing is, "Sometimes when you innovate, you make mistakes. It is best to admit them quickly and get on with improving your other innovations." This quote appeared in the *Wall Street Journal* May 25, 1993, and was preceded by "Being the richest man in the cemetery doesn't matter to me. Going to bed at night saying we've done something wonderful, that's what matters to me." The statement came two months after Jobs' father died, to whom some writers ascribe Jobs' sense of aesthetics.

4. Jeffrey K. Liker and Karyn Ross, *The Toyota Way to Service Excellence* (New York: McGraw-Hill Education, 2017), 46-47. Eiji Toyoda was the nephew of Sakichi Toyoda and a contemporary of Taiichi Ohno, and served as chief executive and chairman of Toyota.

5. Jeffrey K. Liker and Gary L. Convis, *The Toyota Way to Lean Leadership* (New York: McGraw-Hill, 2012), 162.

6. Jeffrey Liker and Karyn Ross report that Toyota used outside call centers to

supplement internal call centers in *The Toyota Way to Service Excellence*. Perhaps this explains, if not excuses, the poor treatment I received.

7. Even though during some discussions with Lean guides the artists expressed an understanding that Lean management approaches were very concerned with the welfare of the people producing work, later in the workshop they still voiced concerns that Lean actions would result in downsizing employment rolls. In the last hour of the workshop, Rebecca, reflecting on the importance of people in theater, expressed a concern with a Lean approach to her work that she could produce a show without props or costumes, but not without people.

CHAPTER 5

OBSERVATION TWO – LEAN, SPIRITUALITY, AND PURPOSE

THE ROOTS OF LEAN

"Lean has its roots in arts and spirituality," stated Rebecca with conviction the third morning of the workshop.

The focus of Lean research and writing is mostly directed at understanding the processes at work in Toyota and elsewhere, and describing them in a manner that allows application in multiple contexts. Less discussed are the historic social conditions that gave emergence to Lean practices. While Taiichi Ohno cites studies in Confucianism informing his opinion on quickly correcting mistakes in *Workplace Management* there is little emphasis on the importance religion played in informing work at Toyota. Christian Wittrock, who has researched the role religion played in the industrialization of Japan, makes a very direct connection between Lean principles and Buddhist and Confucian beliefs. His paper, "Reembedding Lean: The Japanese Cultural and Religious Context of a World Changing Management Concept,"[1] suggests Rebecca saw something many observers of Lean overlook.

Rebecca's statement came during a discussion the artists had with John Shook. Her assessment resonated with others in the workshop. It was voiced during John's description of a diagram he created to illustrate a thirty-year incubation period for the Toyota Production System. [Figure 5.1] There are several dozen influences, including several religious traditions, as well as pioneers in the sciences and humanities. John's diagram includes specific religious traditions including Buddhism, Confucianism, Taoism, and Shinto. There are no explicit references to art in the diagram, so it may be unclear how Rebecca and other artists assessed arts as being a root influence in Lean. While it is easy for non-artists to separate the two—arts and spirituality—for many artists the two are intertwined. Art has a spiritual element, which may draw upon beliefs ranging from a formal religious heritage to a more ambiguous search for an understanding of the spiritual nature of humanity. Native American artist Marilyn Russell argues that art must contain a spiritual quality and that, "art, beauty, and spirituality are intertwined in a spiritual message."[2]

Just as we often see what we are looking for, we often find what we know, so the fact that a group of artists saw "arts" as a primary influence in Lean should come as no surprise. That they would connect arts and spirituality with Lean is significant. While Confucian, Buddhist, and Zen influences are occasionally cited as having influenced the development of the Toyota Production System, the use of spiritual ideas in present day applications of Lean is not widely discussed, because, in its current state, Lean is regarded as a mindset or philosophy without moral consequence.

That Lean has roots in spirituality provides us a sense that beyond

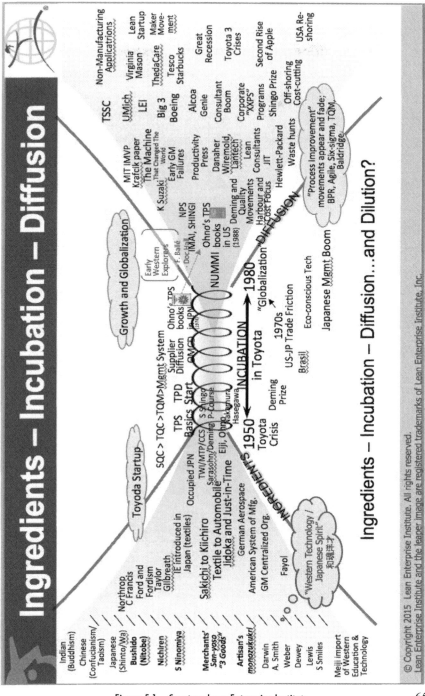

Figure 5.1 - Courtesy Lean Enterprise Institute

working efficiently, or even effectively, Lean draws upon a universal drive to serve a shared, noble purpose. The artists sensed this has been lost. While the thirty-year incubation period at Toyota might have integrated technology and capitalism into older inspirations of a divine nature as the artists suggested, evidence of the influence of spirituality is limited, and as John Shook's chart illustrates, becomes even more diffused as the Toyota Production System becomes disseminated into the broader, and very process-improvement focused, world.

If Lean has its roots in spirituality, then the artists believed that Lean companies might need to challenge some of their fundamental understandings of waste, value, and purpose. In the artists' view, waste, value, and purpose are important; however, none should be viewed primarily through the lens of creating wealth. Their perspective was that while spirituality, American supermarkets, Ford's Highland Park assembly facility, and other influences informed Lean practices that helped Toyota and other enterprises succeed, financial capitalism and command and control forms of authority serve to mutate Lean into unhelpful forms.

Michelle voiced a concern that Christianity may also be an influence that diffuses Lean thinking. By Christianity she was referring to the historic influences of the Roman Catholic Church with its patriarchal structure and authoritarian rituals. She finds the Christian *sheep* metaphor used in Catholic and Protestant denominations representative of ideas that counter some of the religious influences behind the development of the Toyota Production System. In a follow up conversation she conceded this view is subject to interpretation.

In my own interpretation the sheep and lamb metaphors in Christianity are consistent with the religious ideas that influenced Sakichi and Kiichiro Toyoda, Ohno, and others as they developed their approach to work. We need to include a view from the spiritual as we delve into further investigation of the arts perspective on Lean.

The workshop pondered the cynical idea that Lean is not more widely adopted because money, while a consideration in terms of identifying acceptable costs, did not appear to the artists as central to its formation at Toyota. And yet money is central in the current understanding of Lean. By creating value, as defined by the Lean approach, we are creating something worth exchanging for money. By eliminating waste we are eliminating work for which no one really wants to pay. We get excited about productivity gains because it creates monetary gains. Money may be distributed equitably as lower costs, higher profits, and higher wages. Money is a unifier in conversations.

As I wrote the initial draft of this chapter while in an airport lounge, there was a conversation about money in the background. My fellow traveler was expressing her primary goal to make the company as much money as possible so that she can in turn make as much money as possible. Money is a central concern taken for granted by much of the working world. Artists don't necessarily share this concern.

John's slide also illustrates how the process improvement practices coming from the interpretation of the Toyota Production System have diffused over time. These include practices such as Agile, Six Sigma, Lean Six Sigma, Total Quality Management, and Business Process Engineering, along with derivatives of the Toyota Production System at many large enterprises.

It is still too early to know if this diffusion results in a barrier to Lean spreading in a meaningful way or if the less successful practices some call Lean, that actually aren't, will fall away leaving a stronger, core acceptance of this way of working. Christianity offers an example of the latter. The initial spread of doctrine included many different gospels with many contradictions. Ironically it was the imposition of a command and control Greco-Roman orthodoxy on Christianity in the fourth and fifth centuries that helped to cut away diffused messages. It is hard to imagine a similar orthodoxy successfully forming around Lean.

The artists discussed other areas outside Lean in which the influence of spirituality has waned. Michelle commented that music has become highly focused on techniques since the beginning of the twentieth century. Charles Taylor explained how over the last five hundred years the social imaginary, the norms with which we relate to each other, of the west has moved toward a mostly rationalistic and secular stance.[3] It is understandable that the interpretation of Lean that comes from the scientist reflected this rationality and secularism.

The influences behind Lean in John's slide included Henry Ford and Frederick Taylor to represent the production perspective, Charles Darwin, the scientific, and Samuel Smiles for a social perspective. The theological views of Phillips Brooks and C.S. Lewis are not found among Lean influences. Nor is the art of Piet Mondrian or Scott Joplin. This is not a criticism of the slide—it is an observation that the spiritual and arts influences informing Lean are farther in the past than influences from the industrial age and the age of reason.

How did the ideas of people as different as Henry Ford, Samuel Smiles, Charles Darwin, Ninomiya Sontoku, Nichiren, Sakichi Toyoda, and W. Edwards Deming, among others, coalesce into the Toyota Production System? In his book *What Technology Wants*, Kevin Kelly presents technology as a natural, living system. Might Lean, whether as a philosophy or ethic, be considered to be a natural, living system? Does it matter?

There is a case that it does matter, especially if Lean as a living system like agriculture and forested land can be cultivated for the enhancement of human life. That cultivation would be richer if art, as an extension of spirituality, is integrated with the scientific perspective of Lean. It's not as if people have forgotten about either art or spirituality. As Karyn Ross explained in the workshop, plenty of people who fall into the category of the scientist at work have artistic pursuits on the side. There was a sense, shared by the artists and many of the Lean practitioners who participated, that such artistic expression is not accepted in the workplace. This exclusion of the creative arts at work is one practice Karyn, an artist who later became a Lean coach, works to change with her clients.

If arts are barred from the workplace, spirituality is excluded even more so. Conversations about spirituality at work are often uncomfortable. Even during the workshop, Matthew felt compelled to ask permission to include how his relationship with Jesus related to his perspective on Lean. What is fascinating about this reluctance to discuss spirituality is that whether such influences run deep or shallow or somewhere in between for an individual, each person's perspective on spirituality plays an important role in their relationship to humanity. We need to understand those perspectives to fully embrace the *Respect for People* principle, or as in one of its first expressions in English, "respect-for-human system."[4]

The workshop discussion addressed the fundamental question about whether art is for customers, for the artists, or some middle ground. If we are to view Lean as it is about producing work valued by customers, then this is a question that needed to be addressed. What value does art provide and what purpose does it serve? And is Lean even relevant to the art world in this regard?

Jesse posited (perhaps channeling an inner Zen master) that issues of value and purpose may not be a matter of either/or, but they may reside along a unified continuum. Rebecca stated a similar sentiment during another portion of the workshop. This led us to explore the issue of Lean and purpose, and then think about this idea of a unified continuum and how it might apply to Lean. This is a difficult challenge. Vincent van Gogh struggled with a desire for commercial success while holding fast to his way of expressing the world through his painting in a manner that would last through the ages. While much admired now, very few—common lore insists only one—of his more than nine hundred paintings sold while he was alive. Certainly van Gogh never imagined that one of his paintings, *Portrait of Dr. Gachet*, would sell for $82.5 million one hundred years after his death.

Van Gogh's work process was one of continuous testing of ideas for ways to improve his medium of art. Among his inspirations were works of Japanese paintings, in which he saw a spiritual connection between humanity and nature.[5] And like the artists in the workshop, a connection between arts and spirituality.

PURPOSE IS VITAL

The appeal to the artists of arts and spirituality as fundamental to Lean was because they could connect arts and spirituality to purpose. They heard about purpose from some of the Lean guides, and it was central in the video explaining the Lean Enterprise Institute's Transformation Model. The artists appreciated that the topic of *purpose* was part of the discussion.

Some were challenged by the notion that *purpose* in the Lean Enterprise Institute's Transformation Model [Figure 5.2] was the roof supported by the pillars that define the key principles of Lean, which are Process Improvement and Capability Development. On more than one occasion, Michelle insisted that the model was upside down, reasoning that *purpose* needs to be represented as the foundation for work. Michelle later explained that this is because she sees the house metaphor as an active model, and that *purpose*—inseparable from principles and values—must be the foundation upon which the rest of the house is built. Positioning *purpose* as the roof allows for a freer interpretation of what purpose an enterprise or individual might pursue. Thence a shallow purpose, such as maximize profit for shareholders, might prevail.

We did not show the artists the image of the Toyota tree metaphor, and perhaps we should have to see how they reacted. There has been, implicit in the way Toyota operates, a sense of duty, initially to rebuild a nation, and over time, to rebuild the communities in which their employees and customers live. This sense of duty was made more explicit in the image of the Toyota tree metaphor, which Toyota introduced to describe a global vision rooted in principles yielding better cars, and enriching the lives of communities.[6] Crafted for a twenty-first century audience, the global vision excludes any direct language referencing spirituality while emphasizing the importance to the company

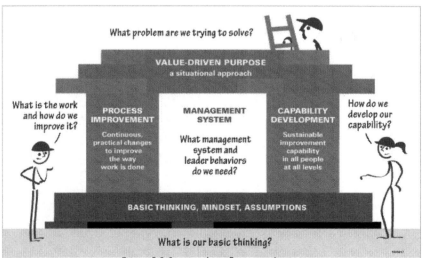

Figure 5.2 Courtesy Lean Enterprise Institute

of enriching lives and respecting the planet—spiritual concerns clothed in secular language.

The artists would not likely accept Milton Friedman's assertion that the purpose of the corporation is to earn a profit.[7] Nor would they necessarily agree with Peter Drucker when he states that the purpose of a business is to create a customer.[8] They would be more inclined to agree with purposes as defined by the Jeffersonian Declaration of Independence. Life, liberty and the pursuit of happiness resonate as more inspired by spirituality than earning a profit and getting a customer.

The artists see the need to connect the purpose of an enterprise with that of the individual, whether working inside an enterprise or as an outside stakeholder. They specifically discussed Steve Jobs as a person who pursued a clear purpose that, in their view, was detrimental to the needs and concerns of others. Kathleen stated that while Jobs was true to his purpose of creating innovative products, he placed people on the bottom rung of concerns. Having a clear purpose can be used to ensure a good outcome, however, if that purpose is disrespectful of people the artists viewed that purpose as detrimental.

The discussion with the artists identified a need for an integration of group and individual purposes. And that group needs to extend beyond the enterprise to the community, leaving three levels of purpose to be integrated. Does Lean facilitate that integration? The artists would say not necessarily the way it is now practiced, but that Lean possibly could if it returned to its roots.

This leaves some important questions. How does social purpose get integrated with individual purpose? How do individuals and groups deal with the likelihood that some group purposes may be at odds with the development of self?

It is important to ask if at the heart of Lean, is there a root purpose—much like the concept of a root cause—very similar to the Stoic definition of the *good life*? What roles do our emotional responses to wonders such as brilliant sunsets, majestic mountain peaks, the seasons, lunar phases, tides, and the stars play in thinking about purpose?

John Shook's slide identifies both a diffusion and dilution of Lean emerging from the thirty-year incubation period at Toyota. Addressing the questions focused on purpose could be a path toward arresting this diffusion and dilution, sharpening the appeal and usefulness of Lean. A spiritually centered purpose, informed by the sensibility of the arts, is the vehicle that positions a creative form of Lean to be more impactful not only on the economy, but also on broader aspects of society.

LOCATING VALUE IN TIME AND SPACE

There is one important feature of Lean that had many of the artists questioning whether the Lean approach to work is applicable to art—the idea that a customer defines value. This idea made sense to those artists who also served in the role of educator. Some expressed a clear sense that the processes and policies of higher education do not always serve the needs of students, who, according to the artist-educators in the room, would be analogous to customers. It was easy for them to envision value from the perspective of a student. At the same time they questioned whether art has such a definable customer.

Related to the issue of who is defining value is the issue of when value is to be defined. Many in the Lean world define the moment value is fulfilled as the point of product or service delivery. Prior to the point of delivery, a producer is creating that value they anticipate will be realized at delivery based on past sales, or in the case of new products, what a combination of testing and research tells them.

In *The Lean Startup*, author Eric Ries describes a Lean approach to developing products and services that customers value.[9] Then there is also the Lean definition of a customer—the person who accepts the work you completed so that they can work on the next step in the processing of the product or service.[10] In this case value is still defined as created at the time of work product delivery.

The artists had a problem with this. They cited many works of visual and musical art created by individuals who were unacknowledged or disdained when they were alive. At the time their work was delivered, it was unappreciated, and in some cases ridiculed. For the workshop participants, the true artist is interpreting observations, external and internal, testing these interpretations, refining them, and sometimes releasing them to the public. The public is not necessarily, in this case, considered a customer as much a player in the artist's creative Plan-Do-Check-Act cycle. Value for the artist is in the learning and not in the final delivery of an artifact. The artists were curious about how Lean might approach understanding this type of value.

They question whether it is possible for art to always be valued by a customer. Perhaps the best art should challenge, disturb, or provoke the customer to move in a direction they may not value. The group discussed commercially successful art, both in theater and in music. Broadway musicals such as *Wicked*, while commercially successful, are not necessarily a valuable form of theater from some artists' perspectives. Popular music is often considered "fluff" according to Michelle, who only recently gave herself permission to enjoy such. Of course none of us in the workshop can know whether in two hundred years some future generation will acknowledge the works of some currently obscure musician as superior to Beethoven, or that musician the heir of Mozart. Contemporary commercial failure in the eyes of learned artists may not always be the harbinger of future veneration.

From the spirituality—and by extension the arts—perspective, value might be considered timeless and may not be realized until many years after an artist's lifetime. As part of the immersion into Lean, the workshop developed the previously introduced notion of a continuum between a timeless value perspective and the market-driven human need for delivering time-specific value.

Jesse and Rebecca specifically addressed the idea of art as standing on either end of a continuum of value. Some art, that which is contemporaneously commercially successful, lies at one end of this continuum. The art that many in the workshop might view as having a higher form, or more truly in keeping with a deeper understanding of the arts, lies on the other end. Jesse asked whether it is necessary to work only on one end or the other. Might an artist choose at different times to work in different parts of the continuum and not necessarily on the ends? Might the artist take on the challenge of spanning the vast expanse of the continuum once they acknowledge its presence?

This model of a value-across-time continuum also served for how the artists thought about who should define value. On one end is the customer. On the other end is the performer. Here it is important to question whether either perspective is ideal other than in cases when the performer and the customer are the same person—an artist who paints for her own enjoyment and learning, for example. Part of the challenge is that each defines value very differently.

We may be defining value too narrowly in Lean, trapped by the notion that value is primarily defined by the exchange of money. While it is true that the customer gains something of value for which we commonly translate into a monetary value, arguably even more value is being created in a Lean enterprise through the process of learning and the development of individuals within the enterprise. And to the degree that individual development aligns with the needs of a society, it is possible that the value created through people development exceeds that of the fiscal output of the enterprise. At best that shows up as "goodwill" in an annual report and doesn't impress Milton Friedman, many shareholders, or the Michigan Supreme Court.[11]

People do practice an appreciation of value that goes beyond that delivered in the present day, escaping monetary valuation. Baked into our laws and customs are practices we value, either for the way they protect our interests or in many cases how they make us feel. We expect a certain ethical level of behavior by leaders, even as some test those expectations. We have an expectation that workers will not be exploited, even as our view changes on what constitutes equitable sharing in the rewards.

What value does a corporation provide? Is it the earnings that feed the next quarterly report and fund the next quarterly dividend? What immediate results are demanded of not-for-profit enterprises and privately owned companies? What might these enterprises provide now that is valued centuries from now? These are the types of questions an artist might ask of enterprises and of individuals.

Recognizing the creation of value that can be sustained across a long period of time is not a foreign concept to aspects of Lean as practiced at Toyota. Long-term thinking has been identified as a principle of Lean.[12] The artists aren't asking for a change to Lean. They are pointing out that the interpretation of Lean, as they heard it, doesn't always align with the ideals they learned about the incubation of Lean at Toyota. It is as if the understanding of Lean remains in draft or sketch form on a canvas. The interpretation of Lean to date has revealed a rough form, but there is more work required to fill in the complete image.

From an arts perspective, the Lean understanding of value is to be challenged and re-interpreted. That's a challenge many people may be anxious to address. Unlike the unveiling of Picasso's completed *Guernica* at the Paris Exhibition of 1937, people will never fully be able to unveil a final vision of Lean. The constructs that we use to inform and interpret Lean will change over time as our perspectives shift. And art should not be the only influence. Maybe as the artists get integrated into the Lean conversation we will find that we also need to invite the theologians to add another layer to the Lean canvas.

1. Christian Wittrock, "Reembedding Lean: The Japanese Cultural and Religious Context of a World Changing Management Concept," *International Journal of Sociology* 45, no. 2 (2015): 95-111.
2. Marilyn Russell, "The Empowering of Art and Spirituality," *Spirituality in Higher Education Newsletter* 3, no, 2 (January 2007).
3. Charles Taylor, *The Ethics of Authenticity* (Cambridge: Harvard University Press, 1991).
4. Y. Sugimori, K. Kusunoki, F. Cho and S. Uchikawa, "Toyota Production System and Kanban System Materialization of Just-in-Time and Respect-for-Human System," *International Journal of Production Research* 15, no. 6 (1977): 553-564, http://dx.doi.org/10.1080/00207547708943149. Published thirteen years before *The Machine That Changed the World*, this paper outlines much of what the IMVP would later discover. The importance of the *respect-for-human system* may have been unappreciated because, as described in this paper, it was a function of Japanese culture and homogeneity. As Toyota would later find with NUMMI and later Georgetown and other factories outside Japan, and as other companies in the United States would learn, the qualities required by the *respect-for-human system* can be cultivated in societies as diverse as the United States.
5. Mark Roskill, ed., *The Letters of Vincent van Gogh* (New York: Touchstone, a Division of Simon & Schuster, Inc., 2008), 295.
6. See www.toyota-global.com/company/vision_philosophy/toyota_global_vision_2020.html for an interactive representation of the Toyota Global Vision tree metaphor.

7. Milton Friedman, *Capitalism and Freedom* (Chicago: University of Chicago Press, 1962).
8. Peter F. Drucker, *The Practice of Management* (New York: HarperBusiness, 2010), 37-38.
9. Eric Ries, *The Lean Startup* (New York: Crown Business, 2011).
10. For an extensive review of how a customer is one of two players in work related interactions in a business process and interactions outside of work requiring agreement between two or more people read chapter 3 in *Conversations for Action and Collected Essays* written by Fernando Flores (North Charleston: CreateSpace Independent Publishing Platform, 2012).
11. In 1919 the Michigan Supreme Court heard a case initiated by two brothers, John Francis Dodge and Horace Elgin Dodge, who collectively owned 10% of Ford Motor Company. They sued the company demanding that surplus accumulated capital be paid as dividends rather than be invested in new plants. Because Henry Ford declared that the purpose of the new plants was to spread the benefits of industry to the greatest number of people, the Dodge brothers requested that the Court prevent Ford from operating the company for charitable ends benefiting employees and customers. While the significance of the Court's ruling is debated, what is noteworthy is the finding of the Court that, "A business corporation is organized and carried on primarily for the profit of the stockholders," and that Ford could not lower consumer prices and raise employees' salaries. See https://pages.law.illinois.edu/aviram/Dodge.pdf to review the Court's ruling.
12. Jeffrey K. Liker, *The Toyota Way* (New York: McGraw-Hill, 2004).

CHAPTER 6

OBSERVATION THREE – THE LEAN VOCABULARY IS INCOMPLETE

LEAN IS A WAY OF THINKING IN SEARCH OF A LANGUAGE

"Lean is a way of thinking in search of a language." When Bryan made that statement, for me, it was the largest surprise of the workshop. I saw Lean as having a very specific language that had largely been developed and interpreted by people with backgrounds in engineering and science. This became the reason why we held the workshop, to discover additional vocabulary to better understand Lean. That someone would appear to find—after several high quality discussions with people who have thoroughly explored and employed Lean practices—that Lean was void a language altogether made me realize that those of us who advocate Lean practices are in a sense speaking in a code most people do not understand. Our background experiences somehow allow Lean advocates an understanding of this code, failing to recognize that our background experiences are far from universal.

Language does more than describe things in the world, it is the way we invent the future. Fernando Flores, an expert in philosophy, cognition, and business, describes this as "the linguistic action perspective," and says our conversations allow us to assess our world, coordinate actions with others, tell stories, develop trust, and shape moods.[1]

Lean has a language. There are plenty of words that describe Lean thinking, Lean tools, Lean practices, Lean management, and Lean philosophy.[2] Conversations are not limited to words. Our gestures and shared use of Lean tools also help us to assess information, coordinate actions, tell stories, develop trust, and shape our moods.

Bryan's comments showed me that, so far, the Lean language has not adequately communicated what some people coming from an arts perspective found relevant. It's not that the artists present were unable to grasp the aspects of Lean being discussed, but they missed seeing the whole picture by a long shot. The role of innovation in Lean is one example. Despite what we facilitators believed to be clear references to how important innovation and creativity are to the Lean process, the artists saw Lean as applied solely to process improvement, and not connected to the act of innovation at all. Kathleen even modeled this perceived divide during the final afternoon. [Figure 6.1] Her model envisions Lean as people busy with process improvement while innovation, represented by a flag and flower, is left untouched by Lean.

The artists viewed the Plan-Do-Check-Act (PDCA) process as a tool to improve production, and did not see innovation as connected to PDCA, despite the fact that in her presentation Karyn Ross had made a point to say that PDCA is at its core a creative process and at the heart of Lean. The workshop participants also had an opportunity to read an article Karyn wrote about PDCA as an artistic process.[3]

Figure 6.1 - Kathleen's process and innovation model

Were the artists listening? Yes, however, what they heard was differ-ent than what the Lean guides had intended to communicate. With-out an expansion of the Lean vocabulary, perhaps informed by an arts perspective, we are limiting ourselves in our ability to use concepts like PDCA, resulting in what Karyn noted as the tendency for people to fall down when it comes to using creativity in the workplace.

When Lean practitioners contemplate the PDCA cycle there is an understood progression from Plan to Do to Check to Act and then on to the next Plan stage. There are many variations of PDCA with different sub-steps sequentially mapped. Kathleen's model of PDCA [Figure 6.2] suggests a different viewpoint. She saw Plan and Check as "towers of stability" and Do and Act as dynamic spaces between these towers. Kathleen may have been responding to John's observation that PDCA allows for ambiguity, and that this ambiguity frustrates scien-tists. Scientists are seeking the answer. This ambiguity is what allows for multiple interpretations from their observations. Artists are better equipped to manage multiple interpretations. Scientists have a differ-ent mindset, reinforced by the ability to use western languages with

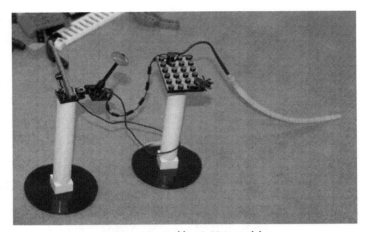

Figure 6.2 - Kathleen's PDCA model

clear definitions and certainty. The use of language, whether by artists or scientists, affects how we think about our world.

Brian Hoffert, PhD, is an Associate Professor of Religious Studies and History, whose research focuses on East Asian history, religion, and philosophy. "Asian languages, especially Japanese, can be far more ambiguous with meaning," Brian told me, "Japanese words are often written in Chinese characters which themselves have multiple meanings layered around the Japanese meanings. Also, in Japan, to maintain social harmony, vagueness is culturally preferred."

This intentional vagueness may contribute to the extraordinary ability of Japanese teams to think effectively in groups because the ideas of any one individual are open to integration with ideas proposed by others. In contrast, within many western teams well-developed and often opposing ideas are brought to the table and debated in what often becomes a battle of egos. Japanese team thinking is more akin to the Lean and creative process of multiple rounds of idea exploration, experimentation, assessment, and refinement. The fact that multiple interpretations of ideas and statements are available is considered a benefit.[4]

In western culture the arts are the domain of multiple interpretations, as is found in painting, sculpture, literature, song lyrics, and even characters in a story—consider how different Frank Baum's characters are portrayed in the 1939 *The Wizard of Oz* motion picture from how they were interpreted for the 1978 film *The Wiz* and in the Broadway musical *Wicked* (2003).

Expression in music opens the door to even broader ranges of interpretation. For example, an online search of interpretations of Lady Gaga's "Bad Romance" produces multiple results—ranging from a theory that the performer sold her soul to Satan in exchange for fame, all the way to the singer's own interpretation that it's about being in love with a best friend.[5]

All these interpretations can exist because the language of the arts presents a rich background upon which our minds can build an understanding of the work being presented, whether or not that understanding is aligned with the intent of the artist. Returning to the topic of innovation in Lean, the disconnect for the artists in the discussion of Lean could not have been because innovation was not covered because it clearly was on several occasions, but that in the language of Lean, innovation is directed toward the foreground of process and getting things done more effectively, not on providing a background upon which people can invent new and better things to do.

John Shook and other Lean guides clearly stated that through its embrace of failure and experimentation, Lean fosters innovation. John also described how a Lean approach to standard work supports innovation. However, the artists did not connect with the words Lean guides were using to describe the relationship between Lean and innovation.

Even in the final afternoon discussion, Kathleen said she saw the Lean process as "wanting to constantly slip into problem solving" and that it caused a "gap in innovation, because it is continually improving what is, but I can't see that as improving what could be."

She was not alone, as the others also had a hard time seeing where innovation fit into the Lean "puzzle."

Bottom line, the current Lean language fails to communicate its essence. After hearing from at least six Lean guides that the *Respect for People* principle precluded using Lean approaches to reduce the labor force, many of the artists still believed that Lean was primarily about cutting labor costs.

The language of the arts is broad and integrates not only emotion, but also the development of psychological states that can be sustained over time, toward intended purposes. But it is the foundational rules and constraints of the process that allow the artist to freely explore their creativity. Only by understanding the rules and constraints imposed by musical keys, color, language, and even physics can the artist experience the seemingly chaotic freedom to experiment and discover new expressions emerging from their creative process. Through process and discovery, they create tension and resolve it (or not), and thus make an impact on the mood and psychological state of the audience.

That there is benefit to Lean enterprises at some level integrating emotional and psychological considerations into the work, work environment, and customer offerings starts to become clear. It's clear we need to start engaging artists in an effort to balance Lean thinking with Lean feeling.

In an earlier chapter I reported on the artists' observation that Lean focuses on delivering value at a specific time, and their concern that value needs to be considered far into the future as well as the present. If we can merge the artist's mindset with the scientist's mindset we can also begin to think about how to work more conscious of the continuum of timeless value and time-specific value that the artists identified. That's a puzzle that the scientific mindset alone may have a difficult time undertaking.

The Lean vocabulary has helped advance people's ability to cooperate and work efficiently to find creative solutions. Still, the language as it stands today lacks the comprehensiveness needed to appeal to a wider audience. By comprehensiveness I mean that the language has gaps, which some people are able to fill based on their previous work experiences. Those people understand Lean because they can fill the gaps and understand Lean as a coherent system of communication.

Bryan clarified that he wasn't saying Lean lacked a vocabulary. He was making the observation that the current vocabulary was insufficient. That the current Lean vocabulary is missing a dynamic element needed to be relevant to a wider audience, as if Lean was the punch line to a joke only a few of us have heard.

OBSERVING FROM THE ARTISTIC PERSPECTIVE

Go-and-see is a fundamental Lean practice. The purpose of going to the work—for example, the factory floor for a manufacturing company or the call center for a customer service department—is to observe deeply, understand the work, and see problems for which an improvement may be possible. We invent possibilities through the conversations we have with others and internally, within our own minds. If our language is limited, then we are also limiting our possibilities for invention.

Artists observe differently than most non-artists. Medical professionals need to be able to observe patients so they can make accurate diagnoses. Programs at medical schools such as Stanford University School of Medicine have been designed to teach observation to medical students through art.[6] These art observation courses are taught in art galleries and are led by arts faculty and graduate students. One of the benefits that the medical students receive is the ability to observe without rushing to interpretation.

David Verble gave the workshop participants very similar advice ahead of the tour of the Toyota factory advising them to observe what was happening without making judgments.

Recall Kathleen's PDCA model, defining the concept spatially, with Plan and Check as "towers of stability" and Do and Act as the spaces where things happen. Notice that the <u>Act</u> space was represented with more transparency than the <u>Do</u> space. Kathleen was representing that a path forward becomes clearer through experimentation. This image opens the door to a new vocabulary with the sense that if we could continue the interpretative work these artists began with toy bricks, then we could make great strides in understanding new ways to compose meaningful and purposeful work.

Artists use the languages of a range of media to observe and interpret life. How might Lean practices be interpreted through music, paint, poetry, sculpture, literature, and theater? If a choreographer designed a dance interpreting a Lean manufacturing process, what can we learn from not only studying the dance, but also examining the emotion and thought that went into the design of that dance? Especially the study of the emotion packed into such artistic interpretations has the possibility of expanding the Lean vocabulary. I propose that we can use experiments like this dance choreography exercise to explore Lean practices, understanding that making work more effective is not enough, and allow work to be more joyful.

Art has many quantitative aspects. The visual arts plays with light waves of varying lengths and shapes with ratios that have been found either naturally or through conditioning to derive more or less pleasing emotional responses. Music is organized in octaves with frequencies that precisely double when moving from one octave to the next. Music and writing both have structures that can be described in mathematical terms. And yet the art is never about the metrics. Art is about the responses, primarily emotional, that people have to stimuli. Art is about the purpose the artist is seeking to explore.

Kathleen said that she did not sense that qualitative experiments were part of the PDCA process. John Shook agreed that is often the case and acknowledged that qualitative experiments are equally, or maybe even more important, than the quantitative ones often favored in Lean processes. Perhaps this is because of the scientific bias for quantitative measurements.

Joanna pointed out that in many cases the artist uses both qualitative and quantitative evaluations when producing a piece.[7] It's in knowing and applying the quantitative that the artist can experiment qualitatively, for example, knowing how scales and meter work quantitatively allows the composer to experiment with sounds that produce a qualitative mood. She emphasized the importance of the artist's ability to engage the world around them from a qualitative stance, observing shape, sound, light, feeling, and color, sometimes connecting these observations with what they know—but often just for the experience. She sees the engineer mindset as being so focused on the challenge at hand that they ignore the world around them, and she believes that this myopic focus limits the information available to them, so they are only drawing upon old experiences when problem solving.

Artists naturally take a qualitative approach to PDCA. They envision their work and create some artifact that begins to make that vision available to others, then, using all their senses, they appraise how well that artifact captures and possibly changes that vision, and then consider what they might do next to bring that artifact closer to its final realization. Adding a qualitative evaluation to experimentation is one area in which the arts can contribute to Lean. While artists ask this question all the time, "How does the experiment make us feel?" this is probably not a question asked in the current Lean PDCA paradigm.

Yet while discussing Lean, it is very easy to focus on metrics and not people and how they feel. Even in Niklas Modig's very human and passionately told story in his *The Efficiency Paradox* video that the artists watched together, we see Lean ultimately expressed as flow efficiency metrics that include reduced throughput time and less waste. The story is about a team of professional caregivers that developed a new way of working to improve the quality and velocity with which they delivered a child's Attention Deficit Hyperactivity Disorder diagnosis to parents and in doing so, cut the time for the diagnosis from five months to three weeks. The numbers are amazing—only because of the emotional impact the changes this Lean approach makes on the children, parents, and caregivers involved. That emotion is easily lost in most conversations about Lean.

Despite a sincere intent to communicate that Lean is about people, it seems, at least with this group, that the human element of Lean did not come across. It is important that when we engage in the Lean practice of "go and see" the work that we include qualitative observations about the people doing the work beyond what we can quantify or even objectively describe. We need to observe with all the senses.

Rebecca discussed how artists use sensory inputs to create psychological states. She shared how actors work using psychological states to adopt certain personas, so as to convince an audience that they are observing the authentic character. This inward reflection helps them capture the qualities of emotion that define that character based on the contexts in which that character must act. It is by observing themselves through the lens of this character and observing the reactions of others that the artist is able to take the next step toward improvement.

The observational language of Lean, even when focused on people, is directed largely toward process and not moods, feelings, or non-verbal cues of the people engaged in the work.

The same applies to how people use language to make observations about purpose. When we defined purpose as delivering some product or service at a given time, then the artists were able to relate the process language to their experience. Michelle needs to deliver a concert by a certain date. Rebecca has to deliver a theatrical performance by a certain date. They both have processes to see that such deliveries are made on time, and Lean practices might help them meet their deadlines with greater ease and efficiency. The difference is they don't see the delivery of the performance as the main purpose of their work. They see performance as a mechanism for the higher purpose of learning through artistic expression—both from their own assessment and the emotional responses from an audience. For them, the performance represents only two parts of PDCA—Do and Check.

People using Lean practices do think about a bigger purpose than on time, on budget production. For example, those tasked with the design and delivery of a medical device that will save lives are aware that by making the device they are participating in the act of saving lives, and saving lives is a noble purpose. And yet the artists did not hear language in any description of Lean that made them think of it as serving any higher purpose. The syntax used to describe a delivery mechanism as one purpose and describing the higher level, noble purpose is the same. Perhaps if we could communicate the access to a higher purpose that adopting Lean provides, we could see it adopted by a broader group of people.

Historically, art has served both social and religious purposes.[8] Even when there may be no intent to communicate a social purpose on the part of the artist, interpretations by others can clothe works of art with cultural meaning. Even those works that Michelle might dismiss as "fluff" can, with a little imagination, be reinterpreted to communicate ideas of social or religious significance. If we look at the observations we make and the language we use to accomplish this act of interpreting works of art we may begin to see a path toward adding a more relevant vocabulary to the language of Lean.

Works of art form a language dialect that we learn over time. Over the last four hundred years we have developed different understandings of the moods major and minor keys in music convey. The reasons for this are cultural, with only a remote possibility that these associations are biologically innate. Any possibly innate interpretations of art can be overcome by cultural conditioning. If we understand the key of E major to be understood as noisy shouts of joy and the key of E minor to be somber it is because our brains have developed associations between musical idioms, scales, and patterns.[9] Music has developed a vocabulary for effecting moods. Joanna used this understanding to help establish a mood conducive to the final day of workshop discussions. She played classical music in the background, later explaining that certain types of music allow the brain to engage more fully while better drawing on memories.

Moods are an important component of continuous learning,[10] and yet the Lean vocabulary does not yet address how we must navigate and cultivate moods in the work environment. The development of this vocabulary is a target rich area where artists and scientists can join forces.

This joint vocabulary will help both the artistic and scientific mind-sets, because there is an opportunity to bridge the gap between the two and permit us to express both our artist and scientist aspects.

As previously discussed in chapter 3, the arts world has its breakdowns. Recall Michelle mentioned the drive some keyboard students have to be among the best sometimes results in compulsive practice sessions, leading to injury, and in extreme cases, destructive breakdowns in which practice rooms and instruments are damaged. Rebecca addressed a related dynamic in theater. Reaching the upper stratum of music and theater is possible for only a portion of the students in top educational programs like that at the University of Cincinnati. To not reach the upper stratum is seen as failure by many students. Both Michelle and Rebecca stated that students need to develop an understanding that practicing their art in places other than in major cities or using their artistic talents in business pursuits is also a valid opportunity for self-expression and growth. Regardless of the arena in which people play, arts or non-arts, leaders need a vocabulary to help learners see rich possibilities. That opportunity is consistent with a Lean ethic, yet we still need to develop the vocabulary for shifting moods in this direction of rich possibility.

WE ARE SHAPED BY LANGUAGE

There are opposing philosophical views regarding the role of language. One perspective is that language is a strict map of impersonal facts existing without human intervention. The other perspective is that language is a creative force that is the vehicle through which humans invent the future. Charles Taylor writing in *The Language Animal* contrasts the enframing, descriptive theory of language with the constitutive theory.

He argues that the former, with its emphasis on language as primarily descriptive coding and communication of information, while useful in a scientific context, ignores how people use language in a constitutive sense to create and coordinate action. The scientist's bias toward seeing language as encoding information versus creating possibilities may be a significant constraint impeding our understanding of Lean.[11] Looking at this model, we can see that the divide between the scientist and the artist is drawn along the same lines. Our inner scientist might prefer language that falls in the first category of impersonal data. Some prefer the Sergeant Joe Friday, "Just the facts," quality, and Lean's language has a strong emphasis on describing and interpreting facts. It's an important quality not to be ignored because observing for facts permits us to describe a part of the world free from uninformed assumptions, but relying on objective, impersonal facts alone is not enough.

Facts must be understood in the context of the observer and the observed. Science supports this position. The observer effect in quantum mechanics is the fact that, on the quantum level, the observer of events affects those events.

A challenge is that many educational systems teach as if we exist in a Cartesian world, in which the universe can be understood with machine-like precision. Students in these systems are rewarded for compliantly feeding back the correct, impersonal "facts" as answers. Joanna declared this paint-by-number educational approach inhibits our natural inclination toward artistic expression. In some schools students who persist with self-discovery through artistic expression are dismissed as "one of *those* kids" and find themselves ostracized. Unfortunately, the separation of exploration and acquisition of two different forms of language begins in schools at an early age. With few exceptions there is little allowance in public schools for variations in learning styles.

Add to this dynamic the integration of machine language to our vocabulary. We drive programs, build organizations, and move the needle on progress. Our homes are machines for living.

The human challenge is framed by Ludwig Wittgenstein's statement that "the limits of my language mean the limits of my world."[15] Facts do not exist outside of language, and if our language is incomplete then so is our understanding of the world. To be clear, when philosophers such as Charles Taylor refer to language, they include words, but also gestures, art, and all tools we use to converse with one another, either directly or indirectly. It may be that in Lean thinking we should not be so concerned with identifying facts as with building a clearer understanding of the world, and how the work we seek to improve upon fits into that world. We need to build a balanced vocabulary.

Understanding the language of art—whether communicated through a painting, literature, music, or theater—provides a path toward expanding our understanding of the world. The language of art is itself dynamic. Whereas art at one time was a reflection of the natural order of things and a description of truth, in the eighteenth century there was a shift toward art as creation.[13] Rather than interpret society's shared understanding of knowledge about God, humanity, and the earth, the artist began to create new language and invent new possibilities. Taylor notes that this is a form of creative expression that involves self-discovery.[14] He writes that "art and beauty cease to be defined in terms of reality or its manner of depiction, and come to be identified by the kinds of feeling they arouse in us."[15]

This is not to say that prior to the eighteenth century art failed to arouse feelings—Taylor's point is that these portrayals were no longer constrained by a social conformity that mandated appropriate feelings based on declarations of impersonal facts. The artists now took more freedom and discovered that they could, through a process of self-exploration, invent a world and share it with others. Arguably this creative process requires a different kind of observational skill, and deeper levels of self-reflection and judgment—capabilities to which the Lean ethic aspires. That this artistic process of creation is not an imperative, and appears to have taken a leap forward the last three hundred years, albeit supported by centuries of technical and intellectual artistic development beforehand, suggests an artistic approach to observation and self-reflection as a roadmap for Lean to break away from a science-centric model of work.

If we are handicapped in appreciating how this important artistic evolution might relate to other work it is because these past centuries have moved our social imaginary toward what Taylor terms the primacy of instrumental reason.[16] In economic applications this results in striving for the most efficient employment of resources toward an end to maximize output. And the reason for the divide to which Rebecca continually referred begins to become clear. [Figure 6.3] While art went down a path of self-discovery and invention, non-art work took

Figure 6.3 The divide between art and instrumental reason

the path of instrumental reason. The Lean intent of *Respect for People* is aligned with the ideals of the artist, which include understanding and inventing a better self. Consider that the way our language expresses this ideal is so married to instrumental reason that new students of Lean hear it as a hollow promise, while the artist can't hear it at all. Thus Bryan's declaration that "Lean is a way of thinking in search of a language."

The experience of the artist workshop suggests that as we further develop Lean, we can learn from the artist's journey through self-discovery and invention, and bring clearer expression to the ideas about work Lean practitioners have been seeking to articulate. I do not recommend that we discard the language of instrumental reason, but that we integrate it with the language of art, and in the process, develop a holistic and healthier approach to work and life.

---

1. Fernando Flores, *Conversations for Action and Collected Essays* (North Charleston: CreateSpace Independent Publishing Platform, 2012).

2. The Lean Enterprise Institute has published *Lean Lexicon*, a glossary last updated in 2014 defining 207 terms. The Lean Construction Institute provides an online glossary of Lean terms specific to the building industry at https://www.leanconstruction.org/learning/education/glossary/.

3. Karyn Ross, "PDCA: The Scientific Method or the Artistic Process?," *The Lean Post* (September 5, 2013), https://www.lean.org/LeanPost/Posting.cfm?LeanPostId=62.

4. The quotation and insights into Asian languages and Japanese culture are from Brian Hoffert, PhD, a professor with a focus on East Asian thought, languages, philosophy, and religion. The statement regarding greater ambiguity in Asian languages aligns with the daily experiences of Joanna McGuffey's aunt, who is a native Japanese speaker.

5. An online search for the interpretation of lyrics for most popular music yields a large number of results, even when the writer provides their interpretation.

6. Jacqueline Genovese, "Honing the Art of Observation, and Observing Art," *Stanford Medicine News Center* (March 6, 2015), https://med.stanford.edu/news/

all-news/2015/03/honing-the-art-of-observation-and-observing-art.html.

7. Joanna's use of the word "piece" to define an artifact produced by an artist is different than the word I have used, "work," as in a *work of art*. My use of *work* as a suitable description may come from a perspective of seeing each individual artifact of an artist as a completed whole resulting from an application of effort. In contrast, the artist sees the artifact as simply one piece of an extended exploration, which may never be finished.

8. Aaron Rosen, *Art + Religion in the 21ˢᵗ Century* (London: Thames & Hudson, 2015), 7-8.

9. Daniel J. Levitin, *This Is Your Brain on Music* (New York: Penguin Random House, 2007), 37.

10. Gloria P. Flores, *Learning to Learn and the Navigation of Moods* (Lexington: Gloria P. Flores, 2016), 29. Moods, Flores notes, as conducive to learning include wonder, perplexity, serenity, patience, ambition, resolution, confidence, and trust.

11. Charles Taylor, *The Language Animal* (Cambridge: The Belknap Press of Harvard University Press, 2016), 33-37.

12. Ludwig Wittgenstein, *Tractatus Logico-Philosophicus*, trans. C.K. Ogden (New York: Harcourt, Brace & Company, Inc., 1922), 5.6. The book was released as an eBook by Project Gutenberg and is available at www.gutenberg.org/files/5740/5740-pdf.pdf. The original statement in German is "Die Grenzen meiner Sprache bedeuten die Grenzen meiner Welt. "

13. Charles Taylor, *The Ethics of Authenticity* (Cambridge: Harvard University Press, 1991), 82.

14. Ibid., 62.

15. Ibid., 64.

16. Ibid., 5.

CHAPTER 7

MOVING FORWARD

THE ARTIST PRACTICES DAILY IN THE CONTEXT OF THEIR IDENTITY

While there are distinctions between how people with artistic and scientific mindsets make observations and interpretations, we must also be mindful that Lean is being interpreted within a social imaginary that resides in the age of reason with a social vocabulary dominated by machine language. Metaphorically our organizations are often compared to machines, and mechanistic properties are used to label social interactions. The machine has no soul, and if it has as a purpose maximizing profits, that is what it seeks, even at the expense of human needs.

At the extreme even our houses have been referred to as "machines for living," beginning with the architect Le Corbusier in his 1927 manifesto *Vers Une Architecture (Towards a New Architecture).*[1] The language of machines favored by our inner scientist allows us to maintain an illusion of certainty. The language of art with its rich ambiguity serves no role in the deterministic framework in which the machine thrives. Our machine language has trapped us in a real life matrix, but the battle is not for an underground Zion or a Skynet-managed future—the battle is for our minds and our hearts.

Borrowing from the idea of the creative ethic, the discussions we held during the workshop suggest that a unification of the language of art and science—through something we can consider to be the Lean ethic—could provide a path toward connecting life and work to meaningful purpose.

The purpose of organizing this workshop was to discover if learning an artistic perspective would contribute to our understanding of Lean. Our discussion with this group of artists supports the view that our reliance on reason in language needs to be augmented with a deeper awareness and appreciation for the ambiguity associated with the artist's creative ethic. Three main observations came out of the workshop.

- Lean has the potential to resonate with the artist's mindset. The practice of Lean begins with the individual and ideally becomes elemental in their personal life, not just their work. Lean needs individuals to cultivate within themselves and model for others a Lean ethic, influenced in part by the creative ethic.

- The Lean roots in spirituality need to be highlighted as a principal driver behind personal and enterprise purpose. Purpose—what do you want to create in the world—needs to be centered on qualitatively measured meaning with quantitatively measured material value playing only a supporting role.

- To expand the language of Lean in a way that makes it more effective and relevant to more people, we need to develop the sensory skills and the vocabulary of the artist and integrate those with the skills and vocabulary of the scientist. This requires that we develop our powers of multi-sensory observation far beyond our current ability.

These observations move us from a model of action that is informed only by reason toward action that incorporates contemplation that is also informed by emotion. These ideas may have been inherent in the way that Sakichi Toyoda, Taiichi Ohno, and their colleagues thought and worked. Some western Lean advocates share ideas similar to those embodied in these observations. Yet even though the ideas informing these observations have precedents, they have not been applied within the Lean community, as small as it is. This chapter provides recommendations on how these ideas, culled from an arts perspective on Lean, can be applied not just to our work, but also to our lives.

The idea that Lean applies to our lives and not just our work is one aspect of the arts perspective that came out in the way the artists talked about themselves. "A pianist—it's who I am!" declared Michelle in the debriefing with David Verble that followed the tour of the Toyota factory. Even though her administrative duties, teaching responsibilities, industry leadership activities, and family interests likely reduce the amount of time at the keyboards to only a small fraction of her day, Michelle's identity as an artist is at center stage.

The suggestion here is not that we strive to reach a point where people declare, "A Lean thinker—it's who I am!" Lean is an approach to work or life, not an identity. Understanding your own identity, and then discovering how to connect the various parts of your life and work by improving yourself and evolving your identity is a creative approach toward life.

Owning a personal identity can be a challenge in many work environments. Professional artists have the luxury of stating their identity as part of their work. Most workers are asked to check their identity at the door. Conforming to the needs of the enterprise can mean setting aside one's personal identity to fit into a job description. The risk being that work and other life demands can become so consuming that one's true identity is forgotten.

A Lean enterprise embracing the arts perspective would find a way to integrate individual identity into the work. This would be achieved by helping us associate how addressing the challenges we face at work can help us address challenges in the other areas of life that matter. Lean teaches not just work skills. In this context, it teaches life skills.

A common understanding shared by the artist and the serious student of Lean is the importance of daily practice. Practice can be individual and can be in teams. Applied to improving the work of an enterprise, practice needs to be both. The next section of this chapter identifies three daily practices designed to help cultivate a Lean ethic, stay focused on purpose, and develop observation skills and vocabulary.

We discussed athletics briefly in the workshop, as one of Michelle's students coaches a professional football team. In addition to daily practice, athletes are given weekly and seasonal cycles. I developed a set of daily and weekly practices I recommend, as well as a set of practices designed to last a portion of the year.

These practices begin with the individual and engage others in the workplace. If you are working in an enterprise that does not support Lean transformation work, begin small with those people around you willing to experiment with ways of making work and life better. As John Shook declared during the workshop, the questions informing Lean transformations are fractal and can be applied at any level from an individual to throughout an enterprise. If you are the leader of an enterprise embarking on a Lean transformation, include yourself in this work. Lean practice cannot be delegated—your own development is as important as the development of the people you lead.

The daily and weekly exercises that follow are suggested as rehearsals that start to integrate artistic performance into our work. Much of life is a rehearsal, and ideally, a search for ways to improve performance. The exercises are intended as a way to invent more vocabulary. This may start with you as an individual, but let your efforts influence the norms of the people with whom you work. This next section suggests practices to create deeper meaning for life's rehearsals.

DAILY PRACTICES FOR CREATING A LEAN ETHIC

Daily Exercise 1:
Developing the Lean Ethic – The Qualitative Daily Plus Delta

For those not familiar with the practice, a Plus Delta exercise is a reflection on an experience. Usually the experience is shared, such as a meeting or training session. As the experience closes the participants voice observations about what aspects contributed value to them, aka a plus, and what change they would recommend to contribute even more value—a delta. The change may add, subtract, or alter an aspect of the meeting.

The practice is part of the Plan-Do-Check-Act (PDCA) learning cycle applied to an experience.

- Plan: The experience was planned. There was an agenda and expected outcome.
- Do: The experience was enacted according to plan, though possibly altered by small PDCA cycles allowing for adjustments to be made.

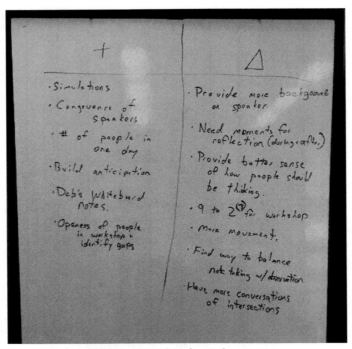

Figure 7.1 – Plus Delta reflection from Day 1

- Check: This is the function of the Plus Delta exercise. The experience is checked against expectations for outcomes falling under the umbrella of providing some determined value for all participants. Deltas are proposed countermeasures intended to result in improving future, similar experiences.

- Act: The people responsible for planning experiences with similar desired outcomes use the Plus Delta feedback to determine which tests to run the next time.

Your day is an experience, and the experience of living each day is one that deserves improving. A daily reflection will help assess what you can do or stop doing, so life moves in a direction aligned with your purpose. Think about one aspect of the day, a plus that added value to your life and moved you toward your purpose. Think about one aspect of the day, a delta, you would change. An exhaustive list of pluses and deltas is unnecessary and not even desirable. One gem of a plus and one insightful delta will take you a long way.

To be effective, this reflection needs to be qualitative. The personal daily Plus Delta is not about counting miles run, calories eaten, sales prospects closed, or LinkedIn likes attained. It's about assessing that aspect of the day that contributed value or joy to your life, and a change you can make that will result in a more meaningful life for you and others. If at first this seems difficult, just start the practice and it will become easier with time.

Daily Exercise 2:
Appreciating Meaning & Purpose – Attention to Awe and Wonder

One of the concerns the workshop members expressed with contemporary artistic work is that inspiration is less prominent than technical proficiency. Kathleen talked about beautifully structured student papers that say nothing of note, with the focus on writing being more about avoiding errors than saying something insightful. The need to inspire people in their work was brought up several times. The group shared the view that we need to approach work with a sense of awe and wonder and how easy it is for that sense to be forgotten.

The following is proposed as a way to awaken the senses to possibilities for creating something spectacular. Pull together a group of five to eight people and agree that each day one of you will find something inspiring to share with the rest of the group. The possibilities can range from reporting a moving act of sacrifice or kindness to sharing a video of an amazing dog trick—though inspirations should generally lean toward the former and occasionally the latter. The sharing can be done electronically to avoid everyone needing to meet at the same time.

The point is to awaken the senses to the extraordinary possibilities for innovation that can be lost to us if we're not looking. This may relate to why the artists failed to see how innovation was a Lean concern. They did not see how the innovation process allowed for the same kind of unusual, unexpected, and extraordinary influences they might look for in developing their art.

Daily Exercise 3:
Seeing with the Artist's Sensibility – Daily Observation Journal

The purpose of this exercise is to develop the many different ways humans have of observing and comprehending the world around us. The journal can be a conventional paper book journal, however, a tablet-based journal will expand your ability to capture observations through photos, video, and recorded speech, as well as writing.

This is different than a standard journal in which people only write observations, thoughts, and ideas. It is also different than an architect's sketchbook in which they draw observations, thoughts, and ideas. In this journal the challenge is to focus only on observation, and to select a different mode of observation each day.

Here is how the exercise works. Go somewhere for five to fifteen minutes. It can be a familiar, private place or a new and crowded one. The place does not matter. What is important is that you observe things about that place and record those observations.

Each day you need to select a different mode to record your observation. One day you might write your observations using words to describe what you see, hear, smell, feel, experience, and perhaps taste. Experiment with using rich, descriptive language that captures the physical sensations and the emotion of being there.

The next day you might draw your observations using images to describe all or some part of what your senses experience. Don't worry if you rarely draw and your drawing skills are poor. The act of drawing your observations is intended to help you see better, and that is what you are accomplishing.

Experiment with other modes of recording your observations. For example, build a model out of clay or toy bricks to represent what you have observed, and photograph that model for your journal. Take a photo or photos of the place and add notes and sketches to the photograph to call attention to your observation. Write a poem. String together four measures of notes. Create a music playlist. Invent new ways to observe and express your observations.

Every day use a different mode to record your journal. Even if you only alternate between writing and drawing you will be developing your ability to see what most people are overlooking. That skill will strengthen your ability for continuous improvement, not only of your work processes but also your relationships.

ARTISTS VALUE EMBRACING A MEANINGFUL PURPOSE FOR THEIR WORK

John Shook's *Ingredients—Incubation—Diffusion* slide specifically includes Indian Buddhism, Chinese Confucianism and Taoism, and Japanese Shinto and Wa as some of the ingredients informing the Toyota Production System. [Figure 7.2] Taiichi Ohno reflects on how his middle school study of *The Analects of Confucius* helped him recognize how conventional manufacturing management attitudes needed to be overcome by applying Confucian principles in *Workplace Management*.[2]

John's slide also includes *Bushido*, a study of the way of the samurai

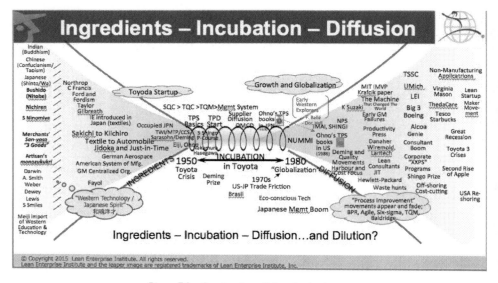

Figure 7.2 - Courtesy Lean Enterprise Institute

as told by Inazo Nitobe, who while Japanese was also a Christian. Themes fundamental to these religious traditions include the transformation of suffering into happiness, internal reserves of courage and wisdom, group solidarity over individual behavior, and harmony in social relationships. In many of these traditions there is the understanding that something bigger than the self is at play.

That does not mean that the individual self is forgotten. The focus in Lean enterprises on helping each individual thrive was one of the most appreciated observations by the entire group of artists, and perhaps most surprising. A challenge they saw is bringing the concerns of the self, the concerns of any given enterprises, the concerns of a community, and the concerns of humanity all into alignment. This suggests another adaptation of the Masaaki Imai Kaizen Framework. [Figure 7.3]

John Shook suggested a modification to the framework that involves Value-Creating Workers in higher-level problem solving. [Figure 7.4] Borrowing John's version of the framework, a continual focus on

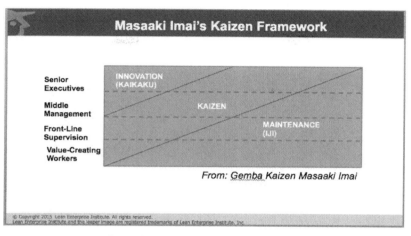

Figure 7.3 - Courtesy Lean Enterprise Institute

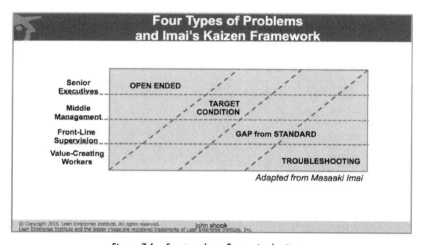

Figure 7.4 - Courtesy Lean Enterprise Institute

purpose alignment may be the most fundamental, open-ended problem that is the responsibility of everyone in the enterprise. [Figure 7.5]

Like a work of art is intended to evoke an emotional response, a purpose for an individual or an enterprise should also connect emotionally. To bring this level of purpose to the workspace is a challenge

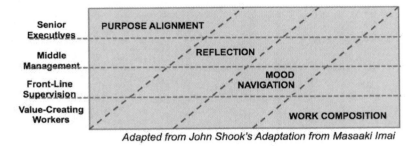

Adapted from John Shook's Adaptation from Masaaki Imai

Figure 7.5 – Purpose alignment is everybody's responsibility

in a culture that seeks positive emotional states and moods through objects. For the enterprise return on investment often serves as a proxy for objects. Often the objects and the returns fail to deliver sustained happiness because they don't touch us in a way that is emotionally satisfying.

Processes related to defining life goals are often reduced to net worth targets, body fat measurements, number of vacations, and opulence of homes. None of these outcomes are bad, and all of these kinds of outcomes can support a broader purpose. But absent the qualitative factor of defining the quality of the experience one seeks, all attaining will fall short of happiness.

When an artist releases a work into the world that work has the potential to provoke others in such a way that contributes to their life, no matter how small, and it may help some community be a better place to live.

This potential for contribution from artwork released to the world is possible because our lives, like art, are more composed than designed. The artist does not stop at design but continues the work through a composition phase. A design is a plan or intention, and a starting place for artistic work. A composition is an invention that uses the artist's arrangement of elements to achieve a unified whole. Finding the best possible arrangement is the result of work, reflection, adjustment, and more work. This distinction needs to be made when thinking about life purpose. Designing a life may be a place to start. We all have intentions. However, we create a richer fabric for life when we welcome the unexpected friendships, opportunities, and adventures in a way that composes a life aligned with meaning and purpose.

Take another look at Kathleen's Plan-Do-Check-Act model. [Figure 7.6] Design happens in the stable Plan phase of the cycle. The unexpected happens while we *Do* the planned work between that stable Plan phase and the stable Check phase. The Act phase is the critical time when we have the opportunity to go beyond design and compose. Very few artists would measure the success of a composition by the money it generated. Money may be a helpful outcome that provides opportunity for future compositions. The artist evaluates a composition against the meaning it generated for their life and possibly the lives of others.

Figure 7.6 - Kathleen's PDCA model

Ultimately for the artists, the work is about composing their life and influencing others as they compose theirs. It is common for artists to seek like minds and build on each other's work. Like the artist, we can develop networks of teams and groups that together form a community unified in the vision of creating a better life for everyone in that community. Each of us needs to encourage individual initiative both within ourselves and in our communities.

WEEKLY EXERCISES FOR COMPOSING WORK AND LIFE

Weekly Exercise 1:
Learning by Helping Others Learn – Weekly Coaching

Select up to three people you can meet with on a weekly basis for ten to fifteen minutes. Ideally, select one person less senior, one person more senior, and a peer for this exercise. Forget about organizational hierarchy when coaching others. Think of the organization as a network of people with different supporting roles. If you are a manager already responsible for coaching and mentoring a group, select from outside that group.

The purpose of these coaching sessions is threefold. One purpose is to help others as they learn to apply Lean skills toward improving some aspect of their work. The second purpose is for you to learn through observing the work of three other people. The third purpose is to more deeply embed a Lean ethic within yourself and the people around you.

During the coaching sessions, review the progress your colleague is making toward reaching a target condition. The agenda for the session is based on the continuous improvement practices described by Mike Rother in chapter 8 of *Toyota Kata*,[3] and begins with a review of the target condition and confirmation it is still valid. Some initial sessions may need to focus on helping the colleague determine a suitable target condition. The time expected to reach the target condition initially should be short, a few weeks to several months. Over time the colleague may want to focus on longer-term target conditions.

Next, review how the current condition changed since the previous week. Then review the obstacles the colleague has identified, and whether they are currently addressing one of them. They should only be addressing one obstacle at a time. For the selected obstacle, review their next step, whether that is testing a countermeasure, investigating causes, or performing an analysis. Finally, confirm what they expect to learn from this next step.

Your colleagues should be cycling through these steps throughout the week as they address improvements they are making. The coaching sessions are a way of making this process a habit for all participants, including you.

Weekly Exercise 2:
Understanding Purpose – Weekly Modeling

Sketch, or using a medium such as clay or toy bricks, make a model of your purpose as you understand it today. Take a cue from the artists who recognized that Lean is rooted in spiritual values and see if this helps develop your purpose in a way that is bold and relevant to you as well as your family, friends, and colleagues. Think about how you might describe your purpose in a way that elicits support from those people closest to you. This is a way of exploring purpose that draws on more than your vocabulary skills. You may find yourself adjusting your purpose as you begin to see it with different eyes. Don't spend long with this. Five minutes is sufficient.

Now, using the same medium, sketch or model the purpose of the enterprise in which you work. Purpose is not something related to revenue or profit objectives. Purpose must be broader and create a value that is timeless. Timeless means not linked to only one point in time, but both immediate and long lasting. Spend no more than five minutes doing this. While the stated purpose of your enterprise may be unchanging, your understanding of it will be different each week, and over time, the way your enterprise lives out its purpose should advance.

Next, take a few minutes to reflect on how the two sketches or models align and where they might not. Consider which areas might need to move into greater alignment and which areas are fine as they are. Think about a small set of countermeasures that might allow work to be more satisfying to your needs and a small set of countermeasures that would help you grow as you better serve the purpose of your enterprise. Pick one countermeasure to test in the next week.

Weekly Exercise 3:
Go and See as an Artist Sees – Weekly Observation

Go somewhere in your enterprise, a customer's enterprise, or a partner's enterprise, and observe people at work. Make sure this is in an area that is completely outside your responsibility—you should be in those places daily. Spend at least thirty minutes observing them at work.

If you can include visits to artists as they work, so much the better. Seek to observe their work—not just the performance but also the rehearsals and practice required for the performance. Seek through observation to understand their perspective on their work.

While you're there sketch or make notes recording your observations. If making notes, give them a literary or poetic quality even if you feel uncomfortable doing so at first. Record sensations such as sight, sounds, smells, and things you can touch or possibly taste. Record the internal sensations you feel being in the place. At the end of the day, review your notes and observations and think about the meaning of those observations for your life and your work.

ARTISTS USE THEMES TO EXPLORE LIFE

Artists use themes to explore ideas about life, society, or human nature. An artist might pursue a theme over varying amounts of time. This exploration can result in an innovation to the art form as a whole as the artist pushes the limits of a medium. With this innovation comes an expansion of the language that all artists gain access to as they go on to invent new work.

Expanding the available language is not only important to better equipping artists. It is also vital to the rest of us, especially as we work to innovate over the long term. Just as an artist explores a theme, we can consider a workplace focus on a particular innovation as thematic—a way of exploring ideas about life, society, and human nature.

Artists invent new vocabulary to expand the possibilities available to them. The Cubism work of Pablo Picasso and Georges Braque required innovation in the exploration of how to represent four dimensions on a two-dimensional surface.[4] In music the sonata form was initiated through the creative work of Emanuel Bach, Joseph Haydn, and others as a fresh way of structuring their works. Before the sonata form could be possible, the five line staff had to be developed, and near the end of the first millennium it was invented as a way in western music to communicate a notation of exact pitches instead of relative pitches. All art whether painting, music, dance, theater, literature, or other forms, continues to invent vocabulary, steadily increasing the story-telling capability of artists. Their works allow us, if we choose, to explore life, society, and human nature in ever expanding ways.

Artists do not invent vocabulary to have more words. They invent to solve the problem of how to better understand and tell a story. The story may well have a lesson, but as Charles Taylor explains, that lesson has very little meaning without the context of the story.[5] Our interpretation of Lean may only be communicating reasoned lessons, explaining why the artists in the workshop questioned whether Lean has a language. What they were saying is, "Where's the story? What are you telling us about life, society, or human nature?"

Lean has vocabulary. There are many words in the Lean vocabulary, with many of them Japanese. Lean also has what are called tools, which are organizational and communication structures designed to continuously improve processes. In practice, they are not truly tools so much as deliberate behaviors. People do use Lean words and behaviors to tell stories. Consider a well developed problem-solving A3. To be able to prepare that document properly, people have explored a problem thoroughly, understood its roots, creatively invented possible countermeasures, and developed a plan to test those measures. There is a story in the work that developed that A3 report. And that story likely fits into a theme, perhaps even developed using a Lean Hoshin form of planning.[6]

Even if we explained the idea that Lean has room for developing themes and stories to the workshop artists more explicitly, they would still respond that Lean thinking needs a language. "Where's the emotional impact?" they would ask. "Where's the development and release of tension necessary to hold attention and communicate the purpose of the work? Why can't we see this purpose by observing the work? Why do we have to see a *Statement of Purpose* hanging on a wall or on the front page of a report?"

I will now connect all three of the primary observations. Applying the arts perspective to Lean we need to cultivate the equivalent of the artist's drive for continual practice in pursuit of perfecting our work. We need to simultaneously cultivate the artist's sense of awe as they develop a purpose for their work that makes a difference in the world. As we do this, we need to cultivate in us the artist's curiosity about their world—a curiosity that observes the world by actively recording and interpreting through their senses.

To cultivate these moods of ambition, awe, and curiosity we will need to invent more vocabulary; and specifically, vocabulary that makes room for the ambiguous interpretations that allow our colleagues, customers, and partners to participate with us in creating work as a form of art. We need vocabulary that helps us not simply enumerate and analyze what work is to be done, but also that emotes the spirit in which the work helps us each become a better people together.

THEMATIC WORK

The following introduces three ways you can develop a theme for your work, and possibly your life. Each requires a consistent focus, so I recommend you employ one of these exercises at a time. These are designed to require several weeks to several months, and might be thought of as similar to sports or theater seasons. Planning for some off-season time will permit you to approach these exercises with greater intensity.

Theme 1:
Model Your Intention to Provide Timeless Value

This is the most difficult of the challenges because it involves creating a model of an emotional state that drives your ambition to realize some greater purpose. This idea comes from the theory of constructivism—the idea that we actively participate in the building of our knowledge structures based on our experiences in the world. Emotional states are built from how we react to certain kinds of knowledge. The objective is to create a model that cultivates a strong mood of ambition.

This is a very personal exercise, and the extent to which you press forward with modeling a powerful emotional future state needs to match your appetite for hard work, experimentation, and risk from an emotional safety perspective. It will test your ability to observe yourself, your surroundings, and your emotional state on a regular basis.

The first step is to select a physical medium with which to work. Drawing works to a certain degree; however, building with the hands immerses the mind more fully into the exercise. As Frank Wilson argues, our hands are not simply mechanical components of our bodies operated by the brain, but are an integral part of how our stories and experiments inform human language.[7] The medium could be clay, wood blocks, or some other material, though LEGO® bricks work especially well given the available variety of pieces and the ease with which they can be assembled and disassembled. You will be using this medium to address a fundamental challenge—how to best represent an ideal emotional state.

There isn't any more guidance to be given about what this model looks like other than to suggest that it is not about having a lot of money, being famous, or achieving prominence in your profession. It probably is much closer to some aspect of your spiritual life or an ideal of service to others. At first you may not know what to build, and that's okay. Just start building. Work on it periodically, but do not let it sit any more than a week without revisiting and reworking the ideas that are informed by the model. When you develop it to a state where the meaning and the future emotional state remain stable, you are ready to set it aside for a while.

One more warning—this exercise is emotionally strenuous and will create tension. You will want to monitor to elevate the level of tension your model creates within you in stages.

Theme 2:
Produce an Artistic Work That Conveys Improving the Human Condition

This exercise is intended to stimulate your creativity and connect it to the *Respect for People* principle. The task is to create a work of art in a medium of your choice. It may be a medium in which you are already practiced, or the work of art may require you to learn a new medium. The medium can be a visual art such as painting or sculpture, or writing such as poetry, short stories, or a book if you are ambitious. Music composition and song writing are other possible choices.

Direct your artistic effort at creating an interpretation of something that improves the human condition. Use the Plan-Do-Check-Act cycle to engage with the work.[8] Each day that you play with the work, *plan* your intention for how you will improve it. Then *do* make those improvements. When you arrive at a stage where you need to *check* the work, consider engaging others to acquire their interpretation and add it to your own. Use this engagement with others as an opportunity to discuss the meaning of not just the art, but also the work you share with colleagues. Then reflect on adjustments you may wish to *act* upon when ready to play again.

Take your time creating this work. This is not a productivity exercise. It is using a different way of thinking to help you observe the world and the role your work plays in making it a better place.

Theme 3:

Focus on Reinvention as Innovation at Work

If you are having difficulty connecting the first two theme exercises to your work, the following exercise will be easier. The purpose of this exercise is to develop an innovation that makes the work of your enterprise improve in some manner. You will still need to develop an artist's sensitivities toward observing and interpreting the world.

Start by envisioning some aspect of work being better one year from now, with better being defined in qualitative and emotional terms. Define the future state of the work as a story with people at work as the characters in that story. Describe what they see, how they feel, and the emotional aspects of their day. Describe the nature of the conversations people have in this future state.

Document the future state on an A3 sized sheet of paper. Do not use bullet point statements. Do not make lists. Do not use a flow, fishbone, or any other type of diagram. Use representative or abstract drawings, poems, or photographs to describe the future state for others to see. Keep your notes about the characters in your future state story in a personal journal.

The A3 future state diagram you share with others will be far more ambiguous than you may be used to developing. That's the point—we truly do not know exactly what we need from a future state until we start to travel that direction. Each step along the way informs us and reshapes how we interpret a future state model only if the model allows for changes in interpretation. Recognize that *true north* is always based on an assessment, and conceptually only exists in two dimensions. Be open to the idea that we live in a four-dimensional world, and that our desired direction may change based on what we learn on our journey. The challenge with future state models that are literal abstractions of ideas is that the abstraction replaces the spirit behind the ideas set to inform the future state. Emotional content is stripped, and we risk losing purpose.

Use your A3 daily to test countermeasures that either bring you closer to your envisioned future state, or help you better understand this future state. The ambiguous nature of the A3 is designed to stimulate measures that bring forth innovation.

ARTISTIC EXPRESSION FOR CONTEMPLATING AWARENESS OF A BETTER LIFE

Throughout history, people have sought kings to direct their work. In the Book of Samuel, the prophet conveys God's warning against kingships. It didn't matter. People still wanted a king. Why would people choose to subjugate themselves to the will of a single person? Perhaps Mark Twain captured the best explanation when he stated, "There are many scapegoats for our sins, but the most popular one is Providence." Whether God, kings, or spouses, having someone else to blame is a common thread throughout human history, beginning with Adam blaming Eve's act of betrayal for a paradise lost. Moses wrote this account. Perhaps Miriam would have told the story differently, blaming Adam for his role in the fall.

The drive for us to install power and responsibility in the hands of a few people who are "above" us persists. Today our kings often have titles such as CEO, Bishop, and Honorable—as in elected politicians. The power of these kings may not be as capricious as times past, however, the vestiges of command and control thinking remain prevalent, and in many cases so does an unhealthy level of disrespect by leaders toward followers, and followers toward leaders.

As an example, a 2012 article reports Apple supplier Foxconn's CEO Terry Gou consulting the director of a zoo to help him manage the one million "animals" employed by the company.[9] It's easy to imagine that this sentiment is shared, even if not voiced, by many other CEOs.

In most enterprises these contemporary *kings,* along with their bodies of court advisors, give directives, which workers follow, even when they know the directives make little sense. In some respects this arrangement is a bargain that works for the kings, their advisers, and the workers. When problems arise each can blame the other, feeling good that they need not take responsibility for causing the conditions resulting from these problems or fixing them. This is a pleasant illusion for some. The reality is captured most accurately in a literary work, Fyodor Dostoyevsky's *Devils,* when Ivan Shatov proclaims his epiphany that, "we are all to blame."[10]

Sometimes this behavior results in fatal problems, killing enterprises, careers, and people. Revolutions, both quiet and noisy, ensue, the power structure changes, and life goes on. And the humans, or apparently animals if you work for Foxconn, involved are no closer to realizing what Stoics would deem the *good life.*[11] They may even be left bereft of any awareness that the *good life* is something worth seeking.

Maybe this is why the artists feel there is a wall between them and the rest of the world. The model Rebecca built showing a wall between the corporate world and the arts world depicts artists as wild animals, representing her understanding of how non-artists view the place artists occupy in a world governed by reason. [Figure 7.7] The artist's passion for noble purposes, beyond what can be rationally explained, is muted. One consequence may be that people are not living with the intention of the *good life* for all. Here is where the artist and the scientist have an opportunity to integrate their perspectives on purpose and work so that the messiness and ambiguity of life and work can be directed toward noble aims.

Spend some time reflecting on how an arts perspective might inspire you to work toward noble purposes for yourself and others. A noble purpose may include high aspirations such as the cultivation of Lean practices within entire communities, so as to enrich the lives of families living and working within.

Figure 7.7 – Rebecca's model of artists and non-artists

A noble purpose can also include just making your corner of the world a bit more enjoyable. One translation from a line in Psalm 104 describes the "leviathan formed for the sport of it." If God can occasionally do something just for fun, so might we. Not every work of art requires a deep meaning assigned to it. Some works can simply be understood to express the joy of being alive, just as we might describe the breaching whale as leaping out of the water for its own pleasure, without regard for any biological imperative that informed the breach. [Figure 7.8]

Niklas Modig in his TEDxSSE *Lean on Yourself* video tells a story about Toyota sensei Hajime Oba being invited to a factory and asked

Figure 7.8 – A leviathan formed for the sport of it

to evaluate whether their operation is Lean.[12] He could not tell them based on this single day because Lean is not a static condition. He would have had to observe their company prior to this visit to begin an evaluation. Seeing improvements through acute observation is the fundamental capability that makes Lean possible. Without being able to observe dynamic changes in the work environment, we have no means of understanding the degree to which *Respect for People* and *Continuous Improvement* principles are at work.

Observation is more than simply seeing. Observation includes all the senses, and an understanding of the feeling and moods informed by the senses. Words, while vitally important, are still abstractions of reality. This is why people have developed and modified practices such as A3 problem solving, 5S visual management, and kaizen events to better understand problems and communicate desired improvements. This practice-based vocabulary, developed through reason and focused on the scientific method, has carried a fortunate group of enterprises forward.

The vocabulary has failed to capture the imagination and harness the energy of the broader spectrum of society. Are we in a prolonged early adopter stage with Lean, or do we need to expand the language of Lean to make it relevant to more people? The artists would argue for the latter.

They might also be tempted to argue for turning Abraham Maslow's pyramid upside down and placing the primacy of satisfying the human need for self-actualization above all else. Without meaning there is little purpose for self-esteem, belonging, security, or even physical survival. More likely they would see any such pyramid as an abstraction; the forced use of reason to explain universal truths too ambiguous to be explained or understood. While this ambiguity may fluster the scientist looking to establish order and certainty, it inspires the artist seeking inspiration for new opportunities of invention.

What should we be inventing? Perhaps it is this thing called the *good life*. The search for the *good life*, while an explicit pursuit of the Stoic philosophers, stretches back to the beginning of recorded history; *good* being embodied in the Hebrew word *shalom* with a meaning that encompasses concepts of peace, harmony, wholeness, prosperity, welfare, and tranquility.

Implicit in the story of the Garden of Eden is the loss of the *good life* following the fall of mankind from a perfect into a broken nature. We've been trying to fix that nature ever since in pursuit of the *good life*, if not for humanity, at least for ourselves.

Oftentimes this pursuit is directed at our work, and Lean has offered a path that when followed diligently has helped many people realize, if not the *good life*, a much better and continuously improving life. It is today still a narrow path, defined by abstractions informed by a centuries-old impulse toward reason that fails to fully engage our world. Understanding Lean from an arts perspective is an initial attempt to widen the path, making it more accessible by helping people observe the world and their work from a more realistic, if also more ambiguous, perspective.

This experiment needs to continue, and several of the people who participated in this workshop are committed to moving this work forward. We know that work starts with expanding our understanding of what it means to observe, and developing an expanded vocabulary based on this enhanced observation capability. We are excited about these first steps toward a more holistic life ethic, informed by the observations that ignited the Lean movement.

---

1. Le Corbusier, *Towards a New Architecture*, 6th ed. (New York: Dover Publications, 1986).

2. Taiichi Ohno, *Taiichi Ohno's Workplace Management: Special 100th Birthday Edition* (New York: McGraw-Hill, 2013). In chapter 1 Ohno comments that, "Engineers, in particular, tend to hold on tightly to things they have said or to their ideas." Ohno appreciated the need to integrate the engineer's desire for certainty with the idea that work is about discovery, which may prove our previous ideas wrong.

3. Mike Rother, *Toyota Kata* (New York: McGraw-Hill, 2010).

4. Susie Hodge, *Pablo Picasso* (Milwaukee: Gareth Stevens Publishing, 2004).

5. Charles Taylor, *The Language Animal* (Cambridge: The Belknap Press of Harvard University Press, 2016), 298-302, 315-316.

6. Hoshin as used here is shorthand for the concept of Hoshin Kanri, a process whereby leaders in an enterprise establish goals, beginning a series of cascading, up and down, conversations designed to align goals with actions able to attain them. It is distinguished from other strategic planning approaches by the approach's engagement of people working at all levels of the enterprise.

7. Frank R. Wilson, *The Hand: How Its Use Shapes the Brain, Language, and Human Culture* (New York: Pantheon Books, 1998), 59-60.

8. While this report has described how the artist's creative approach mirrors the PDCA cycle see "PDCA: The Scientific Method or the Artistic Process?" *The Lean Post* (September 5, 2013) by Karyn Ross for her description of the real "work" of artists. https://www.lean.org/LeanPost/Posting.cfm?LeanPostId=62.

9. Henry Blodget, "Business Insider: Foxcomm CEO: 'Managing One

Million Animals Gives Me a Headache,'" *Public Radio International* (January 19, 2012), https://www.pri.org/stories/2012-01-19/business-insider-foxconn-ceo-managing-one-million-animals-gives-me-headache.

10. Fyodor Dostoyevsky, first published 1871, trans. Michael R. Katz, *Devils* (Oxford: Oxford University Press, 1992), chapter 5, part III. Shatov continued, "and if only all were convinced of it!" He was reflecting on unexpected generosity extended to him during a moment of desperation.

11. William B. Irvine, *A Guide to the Good Life* (Oxford: Oxford University Press, 2009). Unlike a common misperception, Stoic philosophy embraces joyful emotions through thoughtful observation of the world around us.

12. Niklas Modig, *'Lean' on Yourself* (2014), https://www.youtube.com/watch?v=El2e1lxlMGU.

About the Author

Tom Richert is a project and enterprise leadership transformation coach who began his career working on both design and construction teams in the building industry, managing the development of projects in the educational, commercial, entertainment, and infrastructure sectors. He first learned about Lean principles and practices in 1997—practices that corresponded to observations he had made earlier in the study of wastewater and transit economics.

He is a Principal with Lean Project Consulting, Inc., a consulting practice dedicated to improving the experience of project work. His current focus is on helping leadership and project teams develop Lean practices that align with their shared identities and core purposes. This alignment is fundamental to cultivating the mood of ambition necessary to maintain the rigor Lean practices require.

Tom has published papers for the National Research Council Transportation Research Board and the American Society of Civil Engineers; and has lectured at the University of California, Berkeley, and the Wentworth Institute of Technology in Boston. The highlights of the Lean from an Arts Perspective Workshop were presented at the 2017 Lean Construction Institute Annual Congress.

He currently leads coaching programs, workshops, and talks based on the importance of connecting shared team identity with purpose to realize lasting change; a fundamental lesson from the Workshop, supported by ongoing research.

ABOUT LEAN PROJECT CONSULTING

There is a common theme to the work that Lean Project Consulting (LeanProject) does—we transform project-based enterprises guided by Lean principles focused on the human dimension of coordinating work. The firm works in a variety of industries including healthcare, defense, manufacturing, mining and education.

As the demand for the benefits available through Lean practices continues to expand, the firm continues to grow and refine its offerings in the marketplace and it's leadership in the industry. Beyond helping teams implement the proven Lean tools, LeanProject continues breaking new ground, uncovering and inventing new Lean transformational practices, and sharing what we have learned in forums organized by associations that include the Lean Construction Institute, Project Production Systems Laboratory, and the Lean Enterprise Institute.

Whether you intend to implement Lean on a single project, with a single team, or transform your entire enterprise, LeanProject has traveled these paths as a trusted coach before and is ready to guide your people through their journey.

For more information about speaking, workshops, and coaching programs visit www.leanproject.com or send an email message to inquire@leanproject.com.

Made in the USA
Columbia, SC
25 September 2019